ARSENIO HALL

Also by Norman King

Everybody Loves Oprah

Madonna: The Book

Turn Your House into a Money Factory

Big Sales from Small Spaces

ARSENIO HALL

Norman King

William Morrow and Company, Inc.

New York

012093

It is the policy of William Morrow and Company, Inc., and its imprints and
affiliates, recognizing the importance of preserving what has been written, to print
the books we publish on acid-free paper, and we exert our best efforts to that
end.

Library of Congress Cataloging-in-Publication Data

King, Norman, 1926-
    Arsenio Hall / by Norman King.
        p.   cm.
    ISBN 0-688-10827-X
    1. Hall, Arsenio. 2. Television personalities—United States—Biography.
I. Title.
PN1992.4.H347K5   1992
791.45′028′092—dc20
    [B]
                                                                                92-3784
                                                                                CIP

Printed in the United States of America

First U.S. Edition

1 2 3 4 5 6 7 8 9 10

BOOK DESIGN BY M.C. DEMAIO

To Eleanor
My Favorite Sister—My Only Sister
And if I Had a Choice It Would Still Be You

CONTENTS

ARSENIO HALL

1

The Cleveland Connection

Arsenio Hall claims that he is "America's most schizophrenic entertainer." To prove it: "I change every day. One day I have a heart of gold. The next day, I want to march with Al Sharpton the rest of my life."

The Cleveland ghetto neighborhood where he was born was a breeding ground for schizoid behavior and for split personalities. Ironically, it played an important part in inspiring him to do what he did with his life after he worked his way out of its muck and mire.

"Sometimes, I think the most painful elements of my life have created my talk show," he says. "I lived in the house on the corner of a block of projects—the last house they *didn't* tear down."

The conflicted environment in which he lived was dirt poor. "When you broke a window in my neighborhood, it was never replaced with another window." Instead, the empty hole was covered with dry-cleaner's plastic bags stuck into place with heavy masking tape.

Confusion was another manifestation of the area. Although he was born February 12 in the ghetto he has described so graphically above, the year of his birth is far less certain than the day. One year recorded was 1955—the date published in his bio in *Current Biography*. That citation is followed by a question mark.

Publicity released at the time his syndicated talk show debuted in January 1989 described him as about thirty years of age, which would have placed his birth in, say, 1959. But, since he graduated from Kent State University in 1977—the normal graduation age for a four-year college student being twenty-one or twenty-two—he was probably born, as stated in *Current Biography,* about 1955.

His father was the Reverend Fred Hall, pastor of the Elizabeth Baptist Church, located on Holton Avenue in Cleveland. His mother was a health-care worker whose name was Anne, although she was usually called Annie. Annie Hall and the Reverend lived just around the corner from the church in one of the seamier sections of the city.

The rather unusual name Arsenio, which was given to him at birth, has led numerous people to label him as Hispanic, since the name does have a Latino ring to it, but neither Annie Hall nor the Reverend Hall had a drop of Hispanic blood.

When Annie Hall was pregnant, so goes the story, she was seated on an airplane next to a man who was reading a book. In a conversation between them, the man asked Annie if she had thought of a name for her coming offspring.

Annie had not. The man suggested the name Arsenio—a character in the book he was reading. The name appealed to Annie, and later on she discovered that the name was of Greek derivation; it meant virile, coming from the Greek root *arsen*—male or strong. A fitting name, she thought, if she had a boy.

Some weeks later she ran across the same name in a shop window and took that as an omen. She was not a superstitious woman by any means, but she was not entirely oblivious to the importance of *signs*. And so, at the birth of her son some weeks later, she knew that the name was a fortuitous suggestion and christened her baby Arsenio.

In retrospect, it is obvious that her interpretation of the signs she read was right on target. What other Arsenio *is* there in the 1990s?

Arsenio grew up in a household that was in a constant state of warfare between a mother and father who were almost antithetical opposites, another possible source for Arsenio's purported schizophrenic psyche.

The Reverend Hall was a hard-nosed, rigid disciplinarian who had grown up into the mold of a nineteenth-century patriarch. Example: He insisted that his son dress formally for dinner every day. He also had an old-fashioned rule that there would be no dancing in the house. His word was *law*.

In addition, he disliked popular music although he was fairly tolerant of the music of Harry Belafonte, and went in for gospel singing.

Annie Hall was a product of a decidedly different background. She was tolerant of others, and had a solid belief in the dignity of women, which put her always at odds with the patriarchal, Victorian attitude of her husband. Nevertheless she allowed him to demand discipline from their son, even though at times she might think he went too far.

As for her musical tastes, she preferred the *Top 40*—pop tunes that set her foot to tapping. Soul music was fine, as long as it *moved*.

As strong-willed and stubborn as the Reverend Fred Hall was, his wife, Annie, was every bit his equal. The clash of their wills—over music, food, clothing, over Arsenio's upbringing, over everything there was to argue about—kept the atmosphere of the home in constant tension, with the hint of heat lightning crackling in the background.

A generation gap yawned between husband and wife. The Reverend was at least twenty years older than his spouse. It was as if the two of them came from different centuries; in fact, their ideas of discipline *did*. The Reverend was tough-minded and tough-spirited. He was macho, in contrast to his wife's liberated feminism.

Embattled as they were inside their home, they were a closely knit family. They had to be, living in a ghetto patrolled by hoodlums and drug dealers. In order to protect himself and his family, the Reverend had purchased a gun for self-defense. The presence of the gun and the constant use it was put to by the Reverend etched sharp and bitter memories in the mind of Arsenio Hall.

It was not unusual for him to see his father search out that gun at the peak of some argument with his mother and wave it about threateningly. A sense of imminent hostility hovered in the Hall home.

No shots were ever fired. But the threat of gunfire inhabited the place. "It wasn't just screaming," Arsenio Hall says. "It was much deeper and more traumatic. I developed a rash and started sleepwalking"—early manifestations of inherently unresolved conflicts within him.

As his parents continued their verbal and physical abuse of each other, Arsenio took the cue from their aimless running about and squirreled off to where he would be out of range of the seething discontent. "They might find me in the garage in the morning, sleeping in the car."

If the atmosphere within the house was next to unbearable, the atmosphere outside, in the neighborhood of Seventy-ninth and Kinsman, was little better. Arsenio described his street peers as "sophisticated bullies" and recalled one incident:

"This crew of older guys put some dirt in a jar. They came up to me, and one guy took some out with a spoon."

"Try this!" he thundered.

Arsenio shook his head stubbornly. "That's *dirt*, motherfucker." The "sophisticates" seized him and held him tight while the biggest of them jammed the dirt in his mouth.

That was just one of the many events in his youth that cast a cloud over any fond memories of childhood fun and games.

But there were fond memories, in spite of the swirling discontent everywhere. Arsenio shared one of his happier childhood recollections with Oprah Winfrey on her show when he described his neighborhood as a place that "built character." The reason? "You learned to make things for people at Christmas."

And what, Oprah wanted to know, did he remember making for his mother?

"One time," Arsenio said with a bright smile, "I made my mother a kite out of newspaper."

Another thought occurred to Arsenio. His mother was his pal—kind of like a contemporary, not really someone from another generation. "She was like my big sister," he said with a touch of awe.

The neighborhood could either inspire a person to a work ethic—"you learned to work hard to get things"—or it could inspire a person to lie, cheat, and steal. Maybe even kill. Just one more reason for the development of schizoid personalities in its inhabitants.

"I was a very lonely kid," he points out. "I was an only child." In the ghetto, being on his own without real brothers or sisters was a definite handicap. There was strength in numbers, but more than strength was involved. There was *fun* in numbers—fun and games. As an only child, Arsenio felt that his home life left a great deal to be desired.

On the street he had to fight his way out of his solitariness. In the house there was no way to fight loneliness. It was the constant nightly bickering after his father came home that finally led Arsenio to his breakthrough. When the shouting started, he would climb up on the top bunk bed and turn on an old television set. If the bickering continued past prime time, he found himself watching late-night television—which meant the talk shows. And he was soon hooked. Even when the coast was clear and the house was quiet, he would tune in and listen to the conversations between the guests and the host or hostess. *They* became his friends.

When his mother discovered his addiction she was baffled and disbelieving. "What are you watching that silly stuff for?" she asked him time and time again. "That's just talk!"

Just talk! In self-defense, he came up with a plausible reason to tune in. His mother was a serious woman who had to be dealt with seriously. The most serious thing Annie Hall worried about was the future of her only son—that he be able to get out of the ghetto and start a lucrative career.

"I think I could do that when I grow up!" Arsenio said confidently, indicating the set. "I've got to do something," he pleaded. "Maybe I could be like—Johnny Carson."

Annie Hall was not put off by her young son's agile mind. She made him turn off the set and go to sleep. It did little good. After she had left the room, Arsenio simply turned it back on and watched some more. His mother was a good detective, and it did not take her long to learn to check the slit under the doorway for the telltale blue light.

"After I got beat for that once, I learned to put the cover over the TV and my head," Arsenio remembers with a grin. Nothing could stop him from watching the late-night talk shows.

In order to earn a little extra cash to pay for the groceries, Annie Hall would give rent parties—just like during the Great Depression. The idea was to give a party and, in return, keep the admission fee from those "invited" to come.

Arsenio would use each rent party for an audience. He would set up chairs in the basement to emulate the *Tonight Show* set. He would be Johnny Carson. Some kid in the neighborhood would be, say, the "guest athlete."

"He would lift things."

The weight-lifter and Arsenio would discuss where the guest was born, what block, how much he pumped iron, and so on. And maybe even make a joke or two.

But those were the good times. "On other nights," Arsenio remembers, when his mother wasn't checking up on him, "she was being beaten up by my father." Then, of course, she did not bother her son.

"Most people in Hollywood are in therapy," Arsenio muses today. "I'm not in therapy now—but I was when I was five years old. I tripped really hard over their fights."

In spite of the tension and the self-destructive obsessiveness of his parents, Arsenio was impressed, and deeply so, by his father's calling. Fred Hall preached Christian morality every week. Arsenio loved those love-thy-neighbor aphorisms and the way his father rolled them out from the pulpit. He had a marvelous, resounding, hellfire-and-brimstone voice that boomed like thunder.

Arsenio *believed* what his father said about fair play and doing unto others the way you would have them do unto you. What did it matter if he failed to practice it in the confines of his own home? Just another example of the schizoid life-style of the ghetto. It was the oratory and the passion he put into it that intrigued the young Arsenio.

Years later he would consciously imitate his father's gestures and his intonations when he created the role of a bombastic preacher in the motion picture *Coming to America.*

When Arsenio was about five or six, Annie Hall decided that she had had enough of life with the Reverend Fred, and she moved out of the house with Arsenio in tow.

"It happened while I was in school," Arsenio recalls

with a frown. "I came home, my mother took me straight to my grandmother's house, and we never went back."

It was his grandmother's house that Arsenio came to know as home. Sadly—or perhaps inevitably—this home burned to the ground in the seventies while Arsenio was away from Cleveland at college. Nevertheless, in that home, Arsenio's persona was formed—and formed by the presence of women. These two women were independent individuals who had spent their lives getting along on their own—married or not—and it was this fact that made them dominant and dominating. That two independent women were Arsenio's main role models would prove to be an important element in the formation of his outlook on life and on his mode of coping with adversity.

Because of the split between his parents, Arsenio found himself torn between conflicting emotional loyalties. He became what might be called a "knotted sheet" in a personal tug-of-war between his separated parents. This conflict left its schizoid imprint on him.

"There was a time when I wanted a pair of sneakers," he says. When he went to his mother and asked her to buy him a pair, she grumbled at him, by way of excusing herself: "Your *dad* don't do nothing for you!"

Arsenio took that to heart. But intuitively he knew that this might be the loophole he was looking for. And so he did what he could to extract a pair of sneakers from his father, who of course excused himself by shaking his head and muttering a counterpoint to his ex-wife's excuse: "Why should *I* do something for you? *She* got the boyfriends."

To Arsenio the whole episode was a downer. "I was going back and forth over a pair of Coach Converses. I *hated* it. What did her boyfriend have to do with a pair of Coach Cons?"

This tug-of-war over sneakers remained fixed for a long time in the psyche of Arsenio Hall. As a grown man, he has become a shoe miser—stacking his closet with twenty-six pairs of sneakers, twenty of which he never even put on. "I'm a tennis shoe–wearing motherfucker," he admits. "I do wish I could find some Coach Cons, though."

Annie Hall had to work two jobs to earn a living. One was as secretary to a black lawyer named Linden Childs. Childs soon became a kind of neighborhood role model for Arsenio.

"I was just a kid at the time my mom worked for him, but it really impressed me to see this black lawyer, this black man, in a position of prominence and power."

In spite of the presence of his mother's boyfriends and the eminence of Linden Childs, Arsenio still continued to revere the Reverend Fred Hall.

"My father used to tape his sermons, and afterwards he would put my voice on the recorder. I have a library of his sermons I still listen to. My father was either reading the Bible or in his Elizabeth Baptist Church."

And yet the role model was tarnished.

"I would have *liked* a father that took me to a Cavalier game and things like that. I could remember playing catch with my mother and the ball hit her in the head because she couldn't catch. I needed a dad for that."

Still, there was a great deal of the role model in his mother as well. "She has a great sense of humor," he said. It was easy for him to recognize that she was a born humorist when he compared her style of comedy to the talk-show hosts and the way they operated with their guests. Merv Griffin. Mike Douglas. Dinah Shore. And, of course, the champ: Johnny Carson.

Arsenio was much more into his future than the average kid of his day. He meant to *do* something about it even then. "Nobody my age was sitting around all day thinking about Johnny."

He saw something in these gab fests that went to the heart of him. He watched as the hosts and hostesses put their guests at ease in order to bring out the best in them for the viewers. There was skill to it. How did they do it?

Then Arsenio appraised the trick for what it was. It reminded him of watching his own father work the church crowd each Sunday! For that was a host-and-guest situation just like the talk shows.

"I've had relatives tell me that the way I work the stage [now] is just like my dad [worked the Sunday congregation]."

Other considerations were crowding his mind as he watched the TV talk shows. "I was brought up continually being told about how America is a melting pot. But when I watched television, I always saw something missing from that pot. Usually, it was women and minorities."

What he saw on the tube was not really America. It was America as America *wanted* to see itself.

"I couldn't understand why a black artist like Joe Williams, who sang as well as Mel Torme, only got a wave from Johnny [Carson]. Why couldn't Joe tell his stories about touring with Count Basie?"

And that led Arsenio Hall to some serious thought. There was something *wrong* with nighttime TV—talk-show time. There were holes in the talk-show formats. And Arsenio tried to invent one that had no holes, that was *right*.

"I tried to create a show that included black people, that included other minorities, that included all the young people at home who didn't have a talk show to watch. The bottom line is that to enjoy [this show I had in mind] you would have to be open, to accept something a little different from yourself."

He was young, he was eager, and he believed in himself. And that led him to make a commitment early on in life. "When I come through," he promised, "I'm going to make sure I don't mess with little white kids the way this is messing with me." He vowed: "We're going to have a party and *everyone's* going to be invited."

Once he was in school, Arsenio found, for the very first time, a perfect audience: the rest of the class! He knew the jokes. He knew the moves. He knew the way to work the crowd. And almost overnight he became the class clown.

"A lot of people think you get into the class clown thing because you're the funniest guy in the class, or whatever. I was who I was because at home there was no one to laugh at me, there was no one to play with me. For me, it was like, 'Fuck this learning, I come here to party, 'cause ain't nobody at my house.'"

His mother kept telling him, "You're in school to learn."

But Arsenio was thinking, "Later for that, Ma. You want me to learn, have some kids."

Still, he did not quite have the pluck to say it right out.

Even a class clown who wants to be a comic has got to want it real bad to get it.

He wanted it. And he became it. He was the despair of all his teachers. His grades were not at all shameful—in fact, they were rather good. But he had absolutely no respect for discipline in class. Obviously schoolwork cut into the success of his acts.

The teachers in their desperation would write on his report cards: "Arsenio needs attention. Is there anything you can do about it?"

His mother was working most of the time and had by now enrolled in college at night, and even though she tried, she could accomplish little.

"You couldn't get close to him," said Marjorie Banks, one of his Sunday-school teachers. "When you talked to him, he'd see you and yet he didn't see you. His mind was always on something else."

Indeed it was. He was wired to Johnny Carson. To Mike Douglas. To Merv Griffin. To Dinah Shore.

Dinah Shore? "I was probably the only one [in the

city] watching Dinah Shore," Arsenio laughs. In an odd way, Dinah Shore in her role as talk-show hostess served as a definite role model for him.

"You know that graphic at the opening of the show?" He means the nearly illegibly scrawled "Arsenio" that comes on right as the titles begin. "I used to practice that in study halls!"

How had he gotten onto that?

"Dinah Shore used to sign her name like that." And that was what Arsenio used to do—practice signing his own name in that same discursive style—pages and pages of it. "I knew I was going to use it someday!"

All in all, Arsenio Hall tried to be a good boy, tried to act in a way that caused his mother and grandmother little grief. It was a tough life for his mother. He was not completely aware of the stress and strain under which the family of two women and a boy lived.

He came to realize much later that there were times when his mother told him she wasn't hungry—simply because there was not enough to eat in the house. And he came to realize that many times she deliberately stayed away from the apartment until long after Arsenio and his grandmother had eaten and fallen asleep—just so they wouldn't have to share the food with her.

Being on his own like that allowed him to watch the shows he wanted to watch. Frequently, when Annie Hall arrived home late at night she would spot the telltale blue light under the bedroom door and would catch him wide awake watching. It was always the same story.

To take his mind off TV and give him something in line with what he said he wanted to do, she bought him a little tape recorder. The first thing he did was to begin interviews with the neighborhood children. Then he'd play back the tapes to everyone who wanted to hear.

Infuriated mothers soon got at Annie Hall. She could

hear them screaming at their kids: "Stop telling that Arsenio our business!"

It wasn't all fun and games—not in the neighborhood near Seventy-ninth and Kinsman. The neighborhood was an impoverished one, a danger zone, an imperiled area.

Arsenio ticks off the names of high school classmates on his fingers:

"Von is dead, killed in a fight over a girl. Weathersby is dead, killed in an argument over last call in a bar. Freddie's in jail. Jack was picked up for selling cocaine and hanged himself in the prison cell. Tyrone, the star basketball player, is in jail on two counts of murder." One next-door neighbor was shot during a pickup football game.

"Yo, man!" Arsenio shakes his head grimly. "Nobody got out but you!"

By the time he was twelve, he had added a stop-gap "career" to fill in before he became a professional interviewer. "Most kids had a paper route and mowed lawns to make a little money, but I was allergic to grass, so I did magic. My father would do weddings, and I would do magic at the receptions."

He knew that Johnny Carson had started out as an amateur magician—and had added patter to make the tricks go easier. So did Arsenio Hall. He was in junior high school by then.

"I got laughed at a lot," he confesses. "I wanted to do it all, be like Sammy Davis, Jr. But I had to listen to these critics who thought that because I was black, maybe it wasn't in the cards."

There were plenty of people in school who told him *that*. He remembered every detail of every rejection he suffered at twelve—when he almost let his teachers convince him that he should not even bother to apply for college or think about going. That was the closest he ever came to losing faith in himself.

It was Annie Hall who straightened him out. "If you

are going to let them discourage you, I don't want you," she told him, mincing no words at all.

"You remember moments like that," he says. Needless to say, he did *not* give up.

He expanded from magic to magic *and* music. He took music lessons: the drums and the bass guitar. He sweated out the lessons until he was reasonably proficient. Then he branched out into puppetry. He would combine music, magic, and puppetry and hire himself out at birthday parties, bar mitzvahs, and weddings as Arsenio the Magician.

He even got a shot at local television, where he did magic tricks. Just like Johnny Carson!

"I was a drummer and a magician, like Johnny." How his classmates scorned him! He came from the same block in Cleveland as Jim Brown, the football star of the Cleveland Browns. "All the kids wanted to be like Brown," Arsenio recalls grimly. "I wanted to be some little old white guy. I didn't think, as a black man, I was living in the right time."

Further bickering occurred in the schoolyards.

"One day the high school basketball coach asked me to try out for the team. I said no." He told the coach: "I know what I want to do, and I'm not wasting my time. I'm not going to be here after school for basketball practice when I should be at home working on my magic tricks so I can become an entertainer."

School was Club Comedy. School was a captive audience. "Everyone else had nine brothers and sisters. School was my only audience." Teachers used to say, "Arsenio comes to school and he fights to make the class laugh." But they didn't realize what *he* was thinking: "I am here to work this room. I'm here to perform."

Arsenio Hall was an outspoken person. He had the humor and he had the elastic face—the big eyes and the jawful of teeth that even at that age seemed to leap out at you in a flash of red gum and white ivory. He was a handsome young man. Electric. Appealing.

"We had a teacher I used to call Cookie Man, because he used to have those little black marks on his face, like chocolate chips. One time, I raised my hand and said, 'Yo, excuse me, Cookie Man.' I got suspended."

Finally he decided that he might have to settle down and study for a profession of some kind. He chose the law because—as he saw it—there was a lot of talking in the legal profession. Talking to the jury. Talking to the judge. Talking to the client. Talking to himself. And, of course, he had always respected Linden Childs, his mother's lawyer boss.

He admitted later that the lawyer thing was just a smokescreen he thought up to calm down Annie Hall. After all, she could never bring herself to believe that a job in the field of entertainment would open up for her son.

He was accepted by Ohio University in Athens, and he enrolled in the fall after his graduation from high school. Once there he decided to major not in law, but in communications. He pointed out to his mother that communications was a basic course, and he could always move on to law if things pointed in that direction.

Athens was almost a hundred and fifty miles away from Cleveland, in the southeastern portion of the state.

Maybe he'd strike it rich there.

2
Dog Phi Dog

Even though Arsenio Hall found the climate at Ohio University to his liking, he had not reckoned on the amount of time he would spend getting to and from home. His mother wanted him in Cleveland as much as possible, as did his father, whom he saw infrequently but regularly.

And so in due course the young communications major transferred to Kent State University in Kent, Ohio, some thirty-odd miles from the center of Cleveland. He settled into the routine at Kent State as easily as he had at Athens. He seemed to have no trouble pursuing his studies.

At best, Arsenio Hall was outspoken and, at worst, brash.

He stood up in front of a speech class at Kent one day and told his classmates: "I plan on making my living with my oratory skills, and I'd like to be a talk-show host."

"There was a pause," he recalls, looking back, "and then the most incredible laughter you've ever heard in your life. I guess they thought I was crazy. No one stands up in a speech class at Kent State and says he wants to be the next Johnny Carson."

Four years was a long time, but Hall studied for his television and radio communications courses and even managed to dip into dramatics for a bit. He played the lead in the musical version of *Purlie Victorious,* produced at Kent State. Still, Hall's drama counselor once held a discussion with him about his future in the dramatic arts. The counselor was not exactly sanguine about his chances at treading the boards for a living.

"There are audiences and there are stars." The counselor paused and looked his student in the eye. "You were meant to be in the audience."

Undaunted, if a bit discouraged, Arsenio got a job as a disk jockey at the campus radio station, WKSR, and continued to hire himself out as a magician at parties. "My mother still had to carry around all my magician's props when I performed [in Cleveland]."

And then one day Franklin Ajaye came to Kent State to plug his new movie, *Car Wash,* in which he played second banana to Richard Pryor. A stand-up comedian who used nothing in the way of props, Ajaye did his routine on a bare stage as Arsenio watched, bug-eyed.

"Here was this guy on stage just talking," Hall remembers, "with nothing but a glass of orange juice!"

A door to the future seemed to open for Arsenio. "I'm a communications major," he told himself. "I could do this!"

And he began to work on comedy routines, combing the newspapers and magazines for material, and learning how to deliver the punch lines with maximum effectiveness.

He was rushed by the black fraternities at Kent State as a matter of course, but, being a refugee from the Cleveland streets, he turned against the idea of becoming a privileged fraternity man and opted for nonorganizational status. That led in turn to the typical nonorg's amusement at fraternity rituals.

One of the black fraternities had a rite that included a

rooof rooof chant that sounded to Arsenio and his friends like the barking of a dog. The nonorgs got together and founded a phony fraternity they named Dog Phi Dog—and the *rooof rooof* chant was superimposed on the gag ritual.

That chant, according to one story, later became the basis of a favorite Arsenio Hall shtick—the signature of the Dog Pound, a group of special guests present at his television show each night right next to the studio band.

A variation of the Dog Phi Dog story is that Arsenio's chant is derived from the Cleveland Browns football team, where Cleveland fans sit in inexpensive seats called the Dog Pound and express support for their team by barking.

Whatever the source, the chant is distinctive and memorable, and eventually became associated with Arsenio Hall's talk show.

All through his college years Arsenio seemed to be getting further and further away from a study of law. When his father and mother would bring that to his attention on each of his visits home, he would simply pretend that he would get back to *that* later.

It did not work out that way. Arsenio Hall got his degree in general speech in 1977 and was duly graduated with a big senior class at Kent State. Because he knew he had to get some kind of job, he sent out résumés to all kinds of different firms. He knew he had to. Otherwise his mother and his father would both be out after him. His mother was constantly reminding him: "I've got a lot of money invested in that college education of yours."

The job interviews he got were not all that exciting to him. In fact, it was with something like desperation that he finally took a job with a Detroit manufacturing company in the sales department.

The firm was Noxell, the makers of Noxzema and Cover Girl products—cosmetics for the ladies.

Noxell treated its young recruits well. "I had a company car and a dental plan," Arsenio says, "and I was mak-

ing fifteen thousand dollars a year." But that was only the
cake. The frosting? "When women came to my house, I
could give them free nail polish. I was happy!"

Life in the cosmetics trade had its built-in drawbacks.
He found out what it was like being in sales. He would
spend hours of his time sitting around and thinking and uttering profundities like: "Well, the curve of this mascara
brush fits the eye, and I think it's going to do well this
year."

Even during this job stint, he kept honing his stand-up
routine. It was in those years that he perfected the use of
newspapers and magazines as sources for current items to
joke about in his monologues.

"Comedy," he says, "is just like sex. Once you've had
some, you'll live in a small apartment or even a car to get
some more." And the punch line: "And I know a couple
of guys who have!"

He might have stayed at Noxell if it had not been for
The Tonight Show. One night, while he was fretting about
the dullness of his job and the mindless world of salesman-
ship, he tuned in to Johnny Carson to take his mind off his
troubles. He found himself laughing and relishing the scene
on the tube. It seemed more real there in La-La Land with
Johnny than it was in for-real Detroit.

That was the moment he made his final decision. He
knew he had to quit that job and give comedy a decent
shot—even if he failed at it. "I didn't want to go to the
grave saying I'd never tried."

And so the next day, without excessive ceremony, he
turned in his resignation and made plans to move to Chicago, the center of dramatic action for the whole Midwest.
He had to take a shot at show biz. He had to make it somehow as a comic so he could become what he always wanted
to be: a talk-show host.

His mother simply went crazy. "It was one thing to
talk about wanting to be Johnny Carson when I was a kid,

but now she had all this money invested in my degree. I told her that I just didn't want to wake up when I was sixty talking about what I could have been. She wasn't happy, but she went for it."

Wasn't happy? Indeed not. "Don't call *me* if you need money!" she warned him grimly.

But then, in a startling turnaround, she announced that she would be joining him in Chicago once he found a place to live. And she did so. They settled down in a house in Rosemont, Illinois, a suburb of the Windy City. Annie Hall had little trouble getting a job and was on hand to help her son try to break into show biz.

From Cleveland, Arsenio's father wished them the best.

Arsenio did not know what direction to travel in at this point. He knew his ultimate aim was to be a talk-show host, but he did know stand-up comedy and he did know magic. Plus which, he did play drums and bass guitar. But a performer had to be focused on one specific target in order to get it all together. Arsenio Hall had not yet really zeroed in on a proper bull's-eye.

"At that point I was thinking acting and Second City, and then I saw this place called the Comedy Cottage." It was a Rosemont nightclub that showcased embryo comics. "I walked into the Comedy Cottage, and there was a team called Tim and Tom, with Tim Reid from *WKRP in Cincinnati* and the future [*Simon and Simon* and] *Frank's Place,* and Tom Dreesen, the comic who opened for [Frank] Sinatra. And these guys were great."

The scene was intimidating. "I kept signing up to go on, and kept chickening out." In fact, he signed up *eight times* to go on, but eight times never got up onto the stage. Then, on the ninth try, "I finally went up, in Rosemont on River Road, and that night I was hooked."

Needless to say, he did not hit it big right off. But the bonus he won by trying and succeeding—in no matter how small a fashion—was indescribable.

"Once I tried it and got the laughs, no matter how poor, no matter how many bad hotels I slept in, I couldn't shake it." No way. He *loved* it.

He moved on to the Comedy Womb, the Sixty-nine Club, and then on to the discos—the Sheba and the South Side. There, Arsenio would pay the deejay some money to let him do stand-up.

"If I get laughs," Arsenio would tell him, "you double it and pay me. And if I don't, you keep it."

The deejay would object, usually pointing out that he didn't own the place. "I just play records." But occasionally he would take Arsenio up on the wager.

And Arsenio would get laughs, big ones. Sometimes.

"I used to write down my act in notebooks," Arsenio says, thinking about his stand-ups at the Comedy Cottage. "I thought I was pretty good back then, but looking back through those notebooks today, [I can see] I was *terrible.*"

Art Gore, a neighbor of Hall's in Chicago and one of his best friends, said that from the first it was obvious that Arsenio really wanted to get into comedy.

"I can recall him progressing from little clubs, like the Maroon Raccoon Inn just outside Chicago, to becoming the opening act for Parliament Funkadelic, just like that." He snapped his fingers. "He had a rapport with the people," Gore said. "He could adjust his comedy to fit the audience in the club."

Stand-ups did not necessarily stand up on their own. They often introduced other entertainers—especially singers—to the live crowds in the night spots. Because he was into music and was a performer too, he understood musicians and their woes better than a number of his peers.

He found himself reasonably regular work introducing pop singers to all kinds of audiences. And by appearing with fairly big names in the music business, Arsenio Hall began to find himself as recognized and known as they were.

It was then that he experienced his first frisson of fame—that utterly incredible feeling of being recognized by someone he had never met before, just because he was a performer. He had just opened as stand-up comedian—the warm-up—for the Temptations at a 1979 club date.

Patrick Goldstein told about the incident in *Rolling Stone* magazine:

One night Arsenio was riding in a hotel elevator when he noticed that a very attractive woman was more or less coming on to him. In fact, she started the conversation.

"Didn't you open for the Temps tonight?" she asked him.

Arsenio nodded and the woman looked him over from head to toe with *that* kind of a look. "Is there a party?" she asked.

Arsenio shook his head no—there was no party.

The woman was amused. "Could just the *two* of us have a party?"

About this time Arsenio, who had been reacting in a slo-mo fashion akin to an instant replay, finally tumbled to the game. Taking a deep breath, he smiled broadly and said: "Yes."

"We went up to my room," Arsenio recalled, "and she fucked me like she owed me *money*! I kept waiting for her to say, 'We're even.' I mean, this woman didn't even *know* me. All she knew was that I was the sixth Temptation."

In reviewing the episode for Goldstein, Hall shook his head unbelievingly. "I don't know her name to this day! All I remember is that a woman met me in an elevator and because of my performance onstage that night, I didn't have to tell her anything. She just went up to my room and fucked me like she hadn't been with a man in ten years. And I kept saying, 'Shit! I'm a *star*!'"

It was Arsenio's first experience with the physical fall-out that celebrity glamour and notoriety produces in to-day's world.

The Reverend Fred Hall died that same year. Arsenio had continued to see his father even after his mother and he moved to Rosemont, but his father had never really approved of Arsenio's choice of life-style. He had hoped his son would follow in his footsteps and become a minister of the gospel.

However, in spite of his disappointment, Reverend Hall had never written his son off or dismissed him from his life. And toward the end of his days, he seemed to mellow a bit and approve of his son's bent in life.

A few days before he died, he was talking to Arsenio. He said he had just seen Arsenio perform as a magician on a local television station. "I don't care what you do," he told Arsenio. "Just stay close to God. Being a man of God as an entertainer, you'll probably be able to reach more people than I will, and that means something. Whatever you do, strive to be number one at it."

He held up his forefinger and touched Arsenio's with it. Years later, Arsenio would open his nationally televised talk show by touching fingertips with Michael Wolff, his bandleader, in E.T. style. But the gesture was really in memory of his father's reminder always to be number one.

"That's what the pointed index finger symbolizes," he explains with a smile.

A little later that same year Arsenio was signed up to introduce Nancy Wilson, the singer, for her stage show in Chicago on Christmas night. Something happened to the singer's transportation, and she failed to show up at curtain time.

What to do? Arsenio stalled a bit, but finally had to go out on the stage and warm up the audience—with what, he could not even guess.

Wilson did not arrive until after Hall was twenty minutes into total improvisation after he had exhausted his own lead-in material. He was a limp wreck. His act was awful and he knew it. "It sucked."

But Nancy Wilson recognized him as a man of great potential—not only for his innate charisma, but for his ability to make the best out of nothing. And so she waited around after the show to meet him and talk to him.

"He exuded a sense of honesty and warmth," she said, "and I thought he had the ability to be more than a stand-up comedian. He was much better than his material."

"She literally saw me for five minutes only," Arsenio remembered.

But in the end, she told him, straight out: "You have what it takes, and I believe in you."

The upshot of the conversation was that the singer convinced the comedian that he should strike out for the mecca of talk-show hosts—Los Angeles—and try his luck there.

It was through her that Arsenio Hall got an agent and a manager, and he started to pack up a U-Haul to cart his junk out to the West Coast.

He certainly had *not* arrived yet, but somehow he felt that now, at last, he was on his way.

3

Lunch at the Supermarket

Early in 1980 the three of them—Arsenio Hall, his Pinto, and an attached rented U-Haul trailer—arrived in Los Angeles. He had no job. He had very few financial resources. He had nothing going for him but himself, his talent, and his determination to make good.

The first thing he found was that Los Angeles might have been the land of milk and honey, but wasn't that milk and honey *expensive*? Even cheap digs were astronomically, exponentially out of financial reach. He borrowed living space from Nancy Wilson's generous manager and crashed there for a time. Soon he moved into a hotel where he got a room for eighteen bucks a night.

Even food was overpriced. Everything cost more than he had ever paid before.

"I used to eat while I was in—this makes me laugh!—the supermarket. There are a lot of things you can eat while you are shopping. I guess I didn't consider it stealing because I took it out *inside* my body."

In spite of the odds against him, he did survive—and he did even manage to earn a few chances to perform. His

35

first gig was on his birthday, February 12, 1980, when he opened for singer Joe Williams at the now-defunct Parisian Room. He had molded his act by this time so he could not only lead in for a singer or performer, but warm up the audience as well.

His gig at the Parisian Room was the first of many in the coming months and years. In spots all over the country, Arsenio Hall warmed up crowds for major as well as minor stars: Anita Baker. Lynda Carter. Aretha Franklin. Robert Goulet. Tom Jones. Gladys Knight. Wayne Newton. Neil Sedaka. Tina Turner. In all, there were at least thirty major entertainers and many, many more minor ones.

But all the time he was making the rounds, trying to get that all-important—to him—shot on *The Tonight Show*.

There always seemed to be a reason for the "Don't call us, we'll call you" routine.

"You're too barbed," Jim McCawley, Carson's talent scout, told him. "Johnny doesn't *like* barbed."

Arsenio Hall: "I had a joke where I said, 'I watch *Star Search* sometimes, and my question is: "What is Ed McMahon's talent?"' They didn't like that at all."

McCawley said that he liked Hall himself, but found his material sophomoric.

On his eternal rounds Hall collected some affirmative comments, but many were otherwise. He was "too ethnic." He was "too up." He was "too black," "too green," "too animated."He was "too physical." He "moved too much."

He sat down with his manager and the two of them analyzed these so-called findings. Although Hall had always preferred the low-key approach to the high, he found that in southern California's laid-back atmosphere, the Midwest tempo that he considered understated was seen on the Left Coast as hyperactive and disturbing.

The idea was to get some new material and pitch the gags in what was considered the "contemporary style" of entertainment.

"I allowed my manager to hire these writers who could provide material that would get me on the Carson show, get me to cross over."

That was the key term: cross over. A black comic had a problem. Most whites were terrified of blacks—at least subconsciously, the theory went. It was rare that an individual who was black could reach the white audience. Bill Cosby had done so; his fine sense of humor and his superb material helped immeasurably. He had already established himself as a comic personality before his major breakthrough in the television series *I Spy*.

The attempt to cross over cost Arsenio a great deal of aggravation in trying to project what turned out to be a conflicted image—that is, his basic schizophrenia. What was he, really? everyone wondered. A mock Chicago mobster? A southern black? A northern black? An urbanite with a suburban accent? A streetwise Muslim?

At one point, Hall even did a series of Jewish jokes and put on a yarmulke to fit the role! "I had no business doing that stuff," he confesses.

But during the long hard struggle up he used any material he could get and continued to search for new and original concepts that could be tailored to his own special needs. He was close to losing sight of who he was, however, and it rankled him that he could not make it as plain old Arsenio Hall.

"I opened for people I shouldn't have opened for," he recalls. "But Lynda Carter had a show, and I didn't. People knew who she was. And I learned early that the bottom line is not who's the best, it's not color—it's all about green and it's all about butts in seats."

The green was money. Cash on the barrelhead. Bread.

He crisscrossed the country to open for singers. And in his travels he ran across some performers whom he did not cotton to at all. There was, for example, Tina Turner, in Arsenio's view a "nightmare."

"I opened for her at Caesar's Palace in Atlantic City,

1982. She was not a nice lady. She was the only artist I opened for that I never met. Dionne Warwick had warned me about her."

Dionne had asked Tina if she would appear on *Solid Gold,* a television show that Warwick hosted. At the time, Tina had just finished making the movie *Mad Max.*

"Dionne," Tina told Warwick condescendingly, "I'm a movie star now."

Arsenio: "That broke Dionne's face. That chumped her."

With Arsenio, the Turner treatment was in a similar vein. He was scheduled to open for her with his stand-up routine in Atlantic City.

"She sent somebody in to tell me she needed my dressing room to use as a place to receive her guests."

If Arsenio gave up his dressing room he would have no place to make up. "Where am I going to change?" he asked the underling.

"Sorry," was all the underling could say.

Arsenio was sorry, too. He had to dress under the Atlantic City boardwalk on a frigid winter's night.

When he finally met Tina Turner again after opening in his own television show, Arsenio put on a fake, regal, smarmy voice and said: "It's a pleasure to meet you."

Turner nodded, apparently not noticing the irony. "My name is Tina Turner."

"I know," Arsenio said, intoning the words slowly as if to ensure that they would sink in. "I opened for you at Caesar's Palace."

"Oh!" Turner said. "Pleasure to meet you."

And then Turner walked away.

"I think," Arsenio muses, "Ike whipped her ass so much that all black men have come to represent him."

But his gigs were not all disasters for him like Tina Turner's. He was also gaining recognition in the voice-over business. He had a velvet-toned delivery he could call on at will for commercials. He served as the original voice of Winston Zedmore in the cartoon version of *Ghostbusters*.

One of his first big breaks into television came in 1983. Reluctantly, one of the ABC-TV brass decided to take a chance on Arsenio Hall's talent. But it wasn't a clean break-through by any means. It was, as is the custom, conflicted.

"It's time for a salt-and-pepper team to hit, and I don't think you can make it alone," the ABC-TV man told Arsenio in the flossy slanguage of show biz. "So we're going to audition a white guy for you."

And so they brought in people like Wil Shriner and Tom Dressen and Thom Sharp, auditioned them all, and sat back and thought about it. Then they asked Arsenio whom he preferred to work with.

Arsenio decided on Thom Sharp.

"Me and this guy, we didn't know each other from Adam, and they wanted me to do a six-episode summer series!"

It was catchily titled *The ½-Hour Comedy Hour* and was produced by Dick Clark. A short-lived summer re-placement thing—from July 5, 1983, to August 9, 1983—it was on and off the schedule *tout de suite*.

Arsenio and Sharp had a series of regulars on the show, including Barry Diamond, Vic Dunlop, Jan Hooks, Peter Isacksen, Victoria Jackson, Jo Moschitta, and Diane Stil-well. The routines were predictable and generally forgetta-ble: "Bonan the Barbarian," "In Search of the Ridiculous," and "Jennifer Holiday-In." Even Henny Youngman was a guest star, proving that a time warp did exist in television.

Well, the show failed miserably. Arsenio learned one lesson from the exercise and he learned it well:

"Trust only yourself."

"If I ever fail again," he promised, "it will be based on my own sensibilities. I will never, ever let an executive at ABC or Dick Clark tell me what to do again."

As he put it later, thinking about Hollywood and the

types that flourish there: "This town is full of people who aren't talented guiding people who are."

Since the show's life was mercifully short, he was soon released from bondage for better things. The "better things" he came into were perhaps "better than," but nowhere near "best."

It was more than a rumor in the early eighties that Johnny Carson's vaunted Nielsen ratings were slipping. Even though he was still king of late night, he was winding up his third decade on the same throne and his supremacy was not going to remain unchallenged for long. Time for some opportunist to get out the big guns and try to wipe out the king?

The same year the *½-Hour Comedy Hour* fiasco occurred, Fred Silverman, one of television's most astute and famed programmers, decided to crown a new late-night king by removing Carson from the center of the talk-show spotlight. He would do it, he decided, by mounting a spectacular late-night show in syndication—featuring a brand-new star with a brand-new life-style and a brand-new sense of late-night sophistication.

The new host was to be an amiable Canadian performer named Alan Thicke. Thicke had played many roles in television. He was an actor; he had been a producer; he wrote songs; he was not bad at improvisation, either.

Silverman's idea was to provide a show with a looser, more off-the-wall flavor than the rather rigidly structured *Tonight Show*. The format of *Thicke of the Night* was to be similar, of course, but the *tone* would be different.

Alan Thicke got off to a good start, with over a hundred stations carrying the brand-new Monday-through-Friday show. Some of the stations even replaced Carson with Thicke!

Nevertheless, from the beginning, the newly launched vessel foundered. Soon enough it was history—in spite of the energetic rock songs by Thicke and the really funny, zany skits provided by the young comics in the cast—among them Arsenio Hall. The show simply never grabbed an audience, shook it up, and held on to it.

Thicke saw something in Arsenio, however. "I think I recognized that if anyone was going to be the Jackie Robinson of late night, it was Arsenio," he said later. When it was all over and the show was scrubbed, Thicke was anathema, of course. By that time he had earned the dubious distinction of being the Albatross of television.

"I know writers who removed my name from their résumés," he said with a sour laugh. "Arsenio remained a friend in failure, and you learn to appreciate those people in a year like that."

Arsenio was learning things about himself and about the industry. "Hollywood is unreal. This is a town where everyone working in a McDonald's has done a movie." And generally, not a very good one. But how about a movie? Arsenio wondered.

He continued to develop his comic talents in opening gigs during his time off television, but pursued the rounds of the broadcast producers persistently. In 1983 NBC-TV had broadcast the *Motown 25th Anniversary Special,* in celebration of the Detroit-based Motown and Tamla record labels of Berry Gordy, Jr. The one-shot show had proved such a hit—it was top-rated in its time slot—that NBC-TV decided to reprise it in 1985, starting August 9, as a regular weekly show, a kind of musical variety program for the summer months.

From the beginning the show spared no expense in getting the best groups and singers. Many of them were the old-time favorites of the Motown and Tamla record labels, featured for reasons of nostalgia.

Also non-Motown sounds: Boy George. Dean Martin. Linda Ronstadt. Rick Nelson. Weird Al Yankovic. And new artists too: Chaka Khan. Natalie Cole (Nat King Cole's daughter). Vanity.

For host, NBC-TV persuaded Smokey Robinson, a songwriter, singer, and one-time lead for The Miracles, to emcee the affair. He was to act as producer and songwriter for the show.

Among the cast was a handful of young comics who performed their stand-ups between the musical features. Listed at the top of the program was Arsenio Hall.

The reviews were not uniformly marvelous. Quite the reverse, in fact. David Jones, a TV critic on the *Columbus* (Ohio) *Dispatch,* noted:

"This show is a perfect example of how television can turn a beautiful art into 'a viable entertainment commodity' when the wrong people are in charge."

Ultimately, the same critic wrote, it was not the music or the musicians who were at fault, but what was *not* music.

"Every time the music hits a groove, in stalks the ghost of Don Kirshner: Uncle Tom-ish 'comedian' Arsenio Hall, [Lisa] Sliwa, Robinson doing stand-up material left over from Donny and Marie, segue music that sounds like it was clipped from a *CHiPS* car chase."

It had, Jones went on, the atmosphere of a sixteenth-birthday party under strict parental chaperoning: "All your best friends may be there but there's no way it's going to be any fun."

And: "Good times are . . . painfully absent from this show."

It folded on September 13, 1985.

Arsenio Hall did not stay out of the talk-show ring for long. It was in 1986 that he became a cohost again, this time with Marilyn McCoo, a singer who had once been a member of the group The Fifth Dimension. The show was called *Solid Gold,* a showcase for the top ten records of the week—much like the earlier *Your Hit Parade* on radio and television.

Solid Gold had debuted in 1980 with Dionne Warwick as hostess alternating with Marilyn McCoo and several others through the years.

McCoo had left the show in 1984, but returned in the fall of 1986. It was not a network show, but a syndication offering, produced by Paramount Pictures. It was here that Arsenio Hall began fine-tuning his efforts as host.

He also got a slice of excellent career advice during that pivotal year. As a result of his work with McCoo, he found himself opening for her on a night-time gig at the Sands Hotel in Atlantic City. On the same bill was Bill Cosby, whom Arsenio had met briefly once before. About a hundred fans were clamoring to get in to see the star when Arsenio appeared, with the intention of paying him a visit.

The security guard frowned at Arsenio, looking him up and down judiciously. "Who are you?"

"I'm Arsenio Hall, the comedian!"

The guard was about to shake him off when there came a deep rumble from the dressing room where Cosby was changing. The rumble became a discernible voice.

"That Arsenio Hall is no comedian," Cosby called out. "Send that man in here!"

Once Arsenio and Cosby were closeted, the conversation turned to show biz. "Are you happy?" Cosby asked after a few exchanges.

"As happy as anyone can be playing second banana to Marilyn McCoo," Arsenio rejoined.

"If you're not happy doing that gig, why do it?" Cosby asked.

"Because it's a job, Bill."

"I'm going to tell you something," Cosby said. "I don't know the secret to success, but I do know the secret to failure. And that's trying to please other people."

Arsenio did not know quite what to say. He said nothing.

"Do what you want to do, Arsenio," the comedian went on. "There's only one Arsenio Hall on this planet. Please *him*. *Be* him."

He had a chance to put that advice to a test later that same year. Patti LaBelle, who was doing a concert in Los Angeles, had hired Nipsey Russell, the comic, to open for her, but at the last minute he was needed elsewhere. Hearing that Arsenio was available, she called him in to replace Russell.

In deference to LaBelle, Arsenio went to her, figurative hat in hand, and asked, "What would you like me to do and what would you like me not to do?"

LaBelle looked at him, studied him, and smiled. "Honey, that's your act. You do just what you want to do."

Please *him*. *Be* him.

He did Arsenio Hall that night, believing in Arsenio Hall and what he stood for, and playing Arsenio Hall exclusively. He simply let loose with his own special brand of cocky/humble innocent/bawdy badness. The results were astonishing and surprisingly pleasant for him.

"I got my first standing ovation opening for Patti LaBelle because I was being me. And when you come out and they don't know who you are and don't want to see you and then end up giving you a standing ovation, you know you've found it."

Later on, a reporter asked him who exactly *was* Arsenio Hall, anyway? Who was this man that the comedian Arsenio Hall was playing?

"If I tell you who I am, my publicist will go crazy, but I'll tell you anyway. I am an entertainer who was given many talents in many areas so I could do what I'm doing better than anybody's ever done it before. I feel I was born to do it."

And yet there was more to it than just that. There was just a shade of the Reverend Fred Hall there in the back of his only son's psyche.

"At times I've wondered, 'Why me?' Because there are people who are more talented, who are nicer, who need it more, who have worked harder than me. Why me? Then it dawned on me. It's what He wants. . . . My thought is that I'm supposed to do something with it that maybe someone else wouldn't.''

Arsenio still wasn't where he wanted to be—on *The Tonight Show*. Yet every day he continued to hope. And every day he telephoned his mother back in Rosemont, keeping her up-to-date on what was happening to him. After his regular job on *Solid Gold* he had bought her a Nissan Maxima and himself a white Jaguar X-JS with vanity plates: WNERNME (Winner in Me).

The big break, when it came, was not actually a one-shot out of the blue. It was a series of sideways moves that added up to one giant step for Arsenio Hall.

ITEM: One night when Arsenio was getting out of his work clothes and makeup in his dressing room at the Improv on the Sunset Strip, there was a knock on the door.

"Come!"

The door opened and a familiar face peered in at him. Arsenio blinked in astonishment. The visitor was Eddie Murphy, the blockbuster movie actor.

Murphy came in, shook hands with the stunned Arsenio, all the while staring at him thoughtfully. Overcome that he should be visited by such a giant of the entertainment industry, Arsenio could only goggle at Murphy.

Finally Murphy spoke. "You don't look like me."

Arsenio gaped and then burst out laughing. "Who said I did?"

"My mother."

"Your mother?" Arsenio was puzzled.

"She saw you on the tube and thought you looked like me. Actually, she said she thought she was looking at me, because you *acted* like me."

"Are you sure?"

"I'm sure. She said his name was Arsenio Hall."

Arsenio agreed that he was indeed Arsenio Hall.

"That made me want to see you," Murphy laughed.

"And—?"

The long and the short of it was that the two of them struck up a rapport and began—in the words of Arsenio—"hanging out together." They became buddies.

There was more to it than simple friendship. Murphy was the dynamic, up-and-coming black entertainer of the moment, and he had acquired a group of friends. They called themselves the Black Pack—a kind of spin-off of the old Rat Pack that ganged together Frank Sinatra, Sammy Davis, Jr., Dean Martin, and other celebs of the sixties.

The Black Pack was composed of Damon and Keenan Ivory Wayans, late of *Saturday Night Live;* Robert Townsend, the actor, filmmaker, and comic, then appearing in his own film, *Hollywood Shuffle,* and finishing up a comedy thriller later released as *The Mighty Quinn;* Paul Mooney, writer and comic, for fifteen years chief writer for Richard Pryor and also appearing in *Hollywood Shuffle;* Murphy; and now Arsenio Hall.

They worked together as well as played together. For example, it was Townsend whom Murphy asked to direct his concert film, *Eddie Murphy Raw.* Keenan Ivory Wayans cowrote the introduction to *Raw.* Mooney had been the show opener for Murphy on his last concert tour.

Arsenio fitted into the group nicely. But Murphy was the obvious leader of the pack—in influence, in clout, and in the green.

Still, Arsenio's friendship with Murphy was not the breakthrough he was looking for.

ITEM: One night in March 1986, Joan Rivers, who had become a permanent guest host on *The Tonight Show,* was substituting for Johnny Carson. Patti Davis, the daughter of President Reagan, canceled her appearance. Rivers had been impressed with Arsenio Hall after seeing him do several gigs; she thought he had something to offer.

In spite of her knowledge that Carson had nixed Arsenio several times, she instructed the staff: "Get Arsenio

Hall." It was cheeky of her to do it, but she was a cheeky person who used cheek to get what she wanted. Carson's crew knew that the boss did not particularly adore Hall's style of humor, but, after minor quibbling with their guest hostess, they did get the call out to him.

And so he attained *part* of his dream that night. He did appear on the Johnny Carson show. Even though it was opposite Joan Rivers, a substitute for the Great Carson, Arsenio *had* made it. Nor did he ever forget Rivers's generosity that night when she requested him.

His friends in the Black Pack were impressed by Arsenio's appearance with Rivers. After all, Rivers was slated for bigger things. For years Fox Broadcasting, owned by Rupert Murdoch, had been planning to establish a fourth television network—after NBC, CBS, and ABC.

One of Fox's plans was to inaugurate a late-night talk show. From the beginning, it was going to be called *The Late Show,* even though CBS-TV had used that title in the early years of TV with their memorable reprises of old black-and-white movies from the Golden Age of film.

To host *The Late Show,* Fox contracted with Joan Rivers. The announcement of the event was made in the spring of 1986; Fox's debut in the fall would be a major media happening.

The show soon became *The Late Show Starring Joan Rivers.* It premiered in October 1986 in a barrage of publicity and speculation of instant success—not only for the fourth network but for Joan Rivers as well. The show, however, seemed to be not much more than a carbon copy of the basic format: *The Tonight Show (Starring Johnny Carson).*

The long and short of it was that the show simply did not have the drawing power that had been hoped for. Instead of continuing in her brash, brassy, snappish manner, Rivers toned herself down into a kind of verbal drone bent on praising to the heavens every guest she had on. Her

persona was imprisoned somewhere between a rock and a
hard place. Brashness didn't pay the bills. Fawning didn't
either.

So by May 15, 1987, Joan Rivers had left the show.
The title was shortened to *The Late Show* and a rotating
series of guest hosts began to appear. Suzanne Somers was
one of them. Frank Zappa was another. On one of Zappa's
scheduled nights he was unable to appear. A substitute was
required immediately. Fox went through their list of entertainers and began making phone calls.

Arsenio puts it in this typically Arsenio way: "There
were no white people at home one night and I was the only
person they could reach. They looked at my *Solid Gold*
tapes and realized that it might work out. They called me
in and I did it that night and turned it out.

"Everything that was usually done there, I did it a little differently. Everything they expected, I turned it around
to the unexpected."

He walked out and immediately announced: "I hate
the music." He wasn't kidding.

He walked back and started the show all over again
from the beginning. "I said that I wanted the bass
thumping, I wanted the drummers thumping, and I wanted
to hear a James Brown guitar line."

He called out: "Let's do the show like *I'm* here." And
so it went. "I just started breaking a few rules and it
worked out."

Fox invited Arsenio back for a reprise. Once, twice,
three times. By that time, Fox decided that it was a pain
in the neck getting a new host or hostess every night. Why
didn't the comedian sign on permanently as host for *The
Late Show*?

The behind-the-scenes drama at Fox was as good as,
if not better than, the one up front. Fox had doomed *The
Late Show* already and was busily preparing a substitute for
it, called *The Wilton North Report*. But *Wilton North* would

not be ready to air for a couple of months—and *something* had to take its place in the interim.

Arsenio huddled with his manager. In spite of the fact that he had done well in those first rough nights, his manager advised him not to sign on as host on a permanent basis. He would sink himself.

"If Joan Rivers can't cut it," his manager said, "how can a semiknown black kid from Cleveland make a sinking ship float?"

"He didn't believe I could do it." In fact, "Nobody advised me to do that show—except Eddie [Murphy]."

It was Murphy who had said to him: "If they let you do that show one night, the show is *yours.*"

Murphy would be proved right.

So Hall ignored his manager's advice and signed up with Fox to do the show. First for a week. Then for another week. Then for a third week, and so on. Soon the numbers had advanced to thirteen.

"My thing was, get some attention. I took chances. I played with the band, took cameras on the street, did improv, sang, wrote sketches, asked provocative questions, so that when it was over maybe somebody would give me a job."

He had one thing in his favor. He was in with Eddie Murphy, and Murphy agreed to appear on the show. It was said that the Fox studio on Sunset became a kind of Black Pack clubhouse. They hung out in the dressing room, spread out in the audience, did unannounced walk-ons, and even stand-up gag routines.

The night Murphy appeared, the ratings went through the ceiling. So did some of the Fox brass. During the unrehearsed and spontaneous dialogue between Eddie Murphy and Arsenio Hall the two discussed strange women they had dated and had a long talk about penis sizes, among a lot of other unheard-of but zingy things.

Another night Arsenio had on Mike Tyson, who

turned into a kind of teen groupie while Little Richard thumped out boogie-woogie on the keyboard.

On still another, Arsenio held his own against Elliot Gould in a live game of hoop's.

Arsenio invited Emma Samms, of *Dynasty*, to the show, and the two of them rocked the audience with intimacies about each other—intimacies that many viewers thought were verbal hints that the two of them were even more intimate off-camera.

One of the songs Arsenio cowrote with Mark Hudson was titled "We Be Having a Ball." It was used as a signature for the show—and each evening Arsenio started out with the cry: "We Be Having a Ball!"

The song brought in complaints. "We'd get letters from people saying we were perpetuating improper English and this and that. I sat down and thought about it. It's apparent to anyone watching my show that I know correct English. I'm a comedian and this is fun. Anyone who thinks I may *not* know, like say Tommy Hearns or Larry Holmes, they're really not paying attention."

Hall's wild stint on *The Late Show* achieved instant cult status, as if it were a nightly event that you couldn't miss because you knew everyone would be talking about it in the morning.

Bonnie Allen put it this way in an *Essence* magazine article:

"When else had America ever had a chance to drop in on a black living room and see how we really act when we're pretending there aren't millions watching us? For once, no one was editing out the 'Yo, homeboy's and avoiding inside conversation because we were on display. No one was mainstreaming the music and making an effort to appeal to the whitest common denominator. Everybody either got down or got out. This was as real as it gets.

"*The Late Show* was the vehicle that just needed the right driver to get it on the road, and Hall's special brand of affability, humor, and intelligence put things in gear. He had the broad-based knowledge to talk to anybody about almost anything, and the good sense to own up when a subject or guest was out of his league. With flawless instinct for timing he manipulated a barking, hell-bent-for-boogeying audience that could easily have bitten the hand that fed it."

Arsenio continued to innovate. "I was able to do a lot of stuff [on *The Late Show*] because the Fox executives weren't watching," he admitted later. "No one cared."

Certainly Fox did not. Arsenio knew he was doing well by the enormous amount of mail he was getting from new fans. He confronted Fox's program director to find out what the top brass thought about his success.

The program director replied, with a look of total innocence: "You know, [we've been] working so hard on *The Wilton North Report*, I didn't even *know* you were doing this well!" He giggled and continued. "I came down the hall today and saw those bags and I asked what they were and they said they were mail for Arsenio, and I was amazed!"

Amazed or not, the program director did nothing about the evidence. Nor did anyone else at Fox. In spite of Arsenio Hall's resounding success in *The Late Show* slot, the wheels continued to grind inexorably and finally *The Wilton North Report* debuted and Hall was out of a job.

From its opening night, *The Wilton North Report* was an unmitigated disaster. Soon Fox called in Arsenio Hall and asked him to return.

Arsenio surprised them. He said no. What had happened? This:

ARSENIO HALL: One night two execs from Paramount came to my dressing room and said, "We'd like to talk to you about a movie deal." I was ready.

4
The Second Banana

In the early nineteen eighties, while Arsenio Hall was struggling to establish himself as a talk-show host and part-time comedian, Eddie Murphy was already having an almost instant success as a comic on the revived NBC-TV network show *Saturday Night Live.*

In the world of television humor, *Saturday Night Live* was *the* gateway to fame. Started in 1975, the show had fallen on hard times after its main attractions—Chevy Chase, John Belushi, Dan Aykroyd, and Gilda Radner—left to pursue careers in film. In its refurbished state in 1981, a new crew of comics was waiting in the wings, among them young Eddie Murphy.

Immediately Murphy became the major discovery of the recast *Saturday Night Live,* and on the show he expanded his routines and parodies into more complex and integrated affairs. Insult humor was very in, very big. Don Rickles and Joan Rivers reflected the corrosive hostility of the average audience psyche; insults bordered on the cruel, if they did not actually cross the line. Comics could even poke fun at formerly taboo physical attributes and handicaps. Murphy's strength was in creating amusing and believable characters.

Sending up Public Broadcasting's gentle *Mr. Rogers,* he invented a ghetto version called *Mr. Robinson.* His lines became recognizable to a whole new generation of viewers. "Oh, there's Mr. Landlord with an eviction notice," Murphy would say, and the audience would howl.

Among his caricatures was a leucophobe named Tyrone Green (not Black, not White, but Green!), who once announced, "I hate white people because they is white. W-I-T-E." Green then recited his motto: "Kill my landlord. C-I-L-L my landlord!"

One of his audience's favorite characters was a pimp named Velvet Jones. According to Murphy, Jones had just written a best-selling novel that had swept the country. It was titled *I Wanna Be a Ho.*

Murphy did broad takeoffs on James Brown, Bill Cosby, Bishop Tutu. He even did the old *Our Gang Comedy*'s Buckwheat redivivus.

He ribbed Michael Jackson by parodying the singer's soft-spoken, asexual air. He derided Stevie Wonder's lack of physical coordination. And so on.

Because Murphy's targets were wide-ranging, he attracted critical hostility from many different groups, including feminists, as might be expected.

"Eddie, will you marry me?" a woman called out at a concert performance where Murphy was appearing.

"No," answered Murphy. Then, after a short pause, he grinned broadly, gleefully, suggesting in the most obvious way that the woman would have to console herself by favoring him with what *Newsweek* magazine termed "an oral endearment"—i.e., fellatio.

In a takeoff on the old *Honeymooners* television series, he depicted Ralph and Norton as gay lovers. That did not go down well with the real gay-lover set. Nor did a routine with a homosexual Mr. T. Some thought Murphy a rabid homophobe.

But it was in comparison with other black comics of the eighties that Murphy got most of his lumps. Although Richard Pryor had created comical street characters and let loose against sex taboos and fears of race prejudice with barrages of profanity, Pryor seemed to have viewed his junkies, his numbers runners, his winos more sympathetically than Murphy did. Murphy was faulted for not having the affectionate regard for his characters that Flip Wilson had for Reverend LeRoy or Geraldine. Nor did he have Dick Gregory's comprehension of sociopolitical concerns.

At least, so went the criticism.

While Arsenio Hall was still struggling upward, Murphy got his break and made the big switch from television to films. His breakthrough movie was *48 Hours,* released in 1982. In it he was costarred with the enormously talented Nick Nolte, and the plot was a natural: Nolte, a cop, springs Murphy, a streetwise convict, from prison to help him hunt down Murphy's mentally disturbed sidekick before somebody gets killed. Some of the episodes are hilarious, particularly the one in which Murphy single-handedly terrorizes a redneck bar.

It was a sensational debut for Murphy, establishing him as one of Hollywood's top box-office draws. His second picture, *Trading Places,* also teamed him with a white sidekick, in this case Dan Aykroyd. The gimmick of the movie was a switch of the main protagonists in order to test out the efficacy of heredity versus environment by letting a yuppie "have" change places with a streetwise "have-not."

Even bigger was *Beverly Hills Cop* in 1984—in which Murphy pulled the story along all by himself. Martin Brest, the director, was not sure how to handle a sequence in which Murphy's character, Alex Foley, bluffs his way into an exclusive men's club. Murphy came up with the idea of playing "a lisping swish" called Ramon, who waltzes past the maitre d' of the club's restaurant, announcing that he must deliver a message to a member there about herpes, making him a target for the gay activist groups again.

By the late nineteen eighties, Murphy could pretty much write his own ticket with the studios. Now he would dispense with white sidekicks and team himself with another up-and-coming black star—Arsenio Hall.

The story that Murphy wanted was a departure from the old comedy cop routine. Instead, it was a partial rehash of the old Mark Twain story of the prince and the pauper. The prince of an emerging African nation would visit America in disguise as a pauper, a servant to his own servant, who was pretending to be the prince.

The script was crafted by David Sheffield and Barry W. Blaustein, both ex-writers for *Saturday Night Live,* using taped material supplied by both Murphy and Hall.

At the same time the Fox network was thinking of signing up Arsenio Hall as host of *The Late Show,* he was actually signing his name to a contract with Paramount to make the film with Murphy.

Arsenio was not really a newcomer to motion pictures. In 1986 he had participated in a rather unorthodox film venture titled *Amazon Women on the Moon*—an anthology presentation of a number of comedy skits totally unrelated to one another and strung together like a stage revue. So when Paramount needed a director for Murphy's film, it was Arsenio who suggested the name of John Landis.

"I had worked with John on *Amazon Women on the Moon,*" Arsenio said. "I had a lot of fun working with [him]."

Murphy agreed that he too had had a lot of fun making *Trading Places,* which Landis had also directed.

And so it was that Murphy selected Landis for the job of directing the new picture.

In the film, Arsenio would play the character of Semmi, friend and companion to Prince Akeem, Eddie

Murphy's role. Murphy had an idea to hype up the fun in the film. He wanted both Hall and him to play extra roles—three apiece. As Murphy pointed out, Paramount would be getting four actors for the price of one—eight for the price of two.

Arsenio played the second lead, Semmi, Prince Akeem's friend; a ranting preacher spouting aphorisms and gags in a barber shop; a second barber in the shop; and what was described in the script as "An Extremely Ugly Girl" in drag.

Murphy played Prince Akeem; an elderly Jew; a loud-talking barber; and a James Brown–like lead singer of a group called Sexual Chocolate.

The fun in doing the extra roles topped the fun in doing the main characters. Hall was intrigued by the way the makeup man got them up for the scene in the barber shop where there are eight characters gathered at one time, most of them played by Hall and Murphy.

The makeup man, Rick Baker, had won an Oscar for his work in *Harry and the Hendersons,* a 1987 film about a Bigfoot monster encountered in the woods and taken home by a family as a pet.

"Well," Arsenio told a reporter, "Rick Baker sat down with us and looked at us and studied us and took pictures."

Then he announced: "Now, Arsenio, you have a huge smile and tiny ears. These are the things we're going to work on the most."

"As the barber," Arsenio said, "I got a different nose and teeth and a beard—and, well, it all took about an hour and a half to turn me into the barber."

The preacher was harder. "It took them four hours doing the preacher on me. Every part of my face was different. But I liked being Reverend Brown because my father was a Baptist preacher, and it gave me a chance to use all those things I'd observed him doing. I'll tell you, he could cry on command, just like Jimmy Swaggart."

As the Extremely Ugly Woman, Arsenio recalled: "I put on the hose and the girdle and everything. And it really freaked Eddie out. He wouldn't do another take."

The story itself is viable—barely. It starts in the mythical African kingdom of Zamunda. Prince Akeem has everything: beautiful women to bathe him in the morning, barns full of winning polo ponies, more money than Donald Trump had when he had it. Yet for some reason Akeem wants out.

His father the king—James Earl Jones—arranges for a standard beauty to marry the prince. Akeem demurs. He's bored with his life of luxury. He wants to see the world.

"I understand, my son," booms out King Jones in his patented voice-over manner. "You want to sow your royal oats."

The deal is struck. Akeem and Semmi will go to America.

"Forty days and forty nights," says Akeem thoughtfully, "of meditation."

Semmi's eyes gleam as only Arsenio can make eyes gleam. "Forty days of fornication!" he corrects ecstatically.

Then the truth comes out. Akeem wants to marry an American woman. "I want someone who thinks for herself," he tells Semmi.

They land in a typical Queens neighborhood and Akeem launches his search for a bride. The prince, playing the pauper, takes a job sweeping the floor of a hamburger joint. He's been struck by the sight of the boss's daughter, Lisa.

Vanished is the foul-mouthed, streetwise, arrogant Eddie Murphy, replaced by a cuddly, warm, lovey-dovey fellow who goes mushy at the sight of the girl of his dreams. It is, in fact, Arsenio as Semmi who provides the cutting edge to the story. When it's all over and the king and queen arrive to hunt down Prince Akeem and take the entourage back to Zamunda, Hall looks philosophical and says: "At least we learned how to make french fries."

Arsenio's experience in making the film with Murphy was not the enchanting diversion he had hoped for. As he told Digby Diehl in a *Cosmopolitan* magazine interview, "I found out that I hate to do movies. It was a nightmare. Making movies is very complicated, tedious, and tiresome. It is especially terrible for a comic, because you do a joke and you turn to people and ask, 'Was it funny?' They say, 'We'll let you know in eight months.' I wanted to get back into TV—badly."

Ironically, John Landis seemed to have been the main reason Arsenio disliked working in films. Arsenio confessed that both he and Murphy had vowed never to make another picture with the director.

"Chevy Chase once described Landis as 'an attack dog on a leash,'" Arsenio said. "I felt like I was playing tag. My life was in Landis's hands—because I'm the one nude sitting in the tub in front of the camera. It's *trust.*"

As for Murphy's misguided enthusiasm for Landis, evoked by the fun he had working on *Trading Places,* Arsenio explained: "When Eddie made *Trading Places* he was a young boy. When he came to make this movie, he was the number one box-office star—and John didn't treat him any differently."

Another thing that bothered Arsenio was that he never got a chance to see any of the rushes—the daily film clips that show how the picture is progressing. Landis himself explained why he never let his actors see the rushes.

"I've been directing too long to allow an actor to watch himself during filming," he told Gerri Hirshey of *Vanity Fair.* "If they see something they like—or, worse, something they don't like—it can be hell the next day on the set."

Arsenio was awestruck at playing a scene with James Earl Jones, whom he had long admired but had never met. Jones was most generous in showing Arsenio how to find his mark for the shot and even laughing during their first scene together when Arsenio stopped the filming, as he said, "from the sheer awe of the moment."

One of the scenes in the picture took place in a tenement in Queens. Arsenio was supposed to wake up to see a rat on his bed.

"I couldn't handle it," he admitted. "Not even a fake rat, which they also tried. When I was a kid in Cleveland—I was five—I was sitting on the toilet and a rat ran across my foot. And it's weird, I decided right then, sitting there terrified out of my mind, that my big goal was to live in a house with no rats and roaches someday. Me and my mother. That's all I wanted."

In spite of the memories that the scene inspired in Arsenio, he did a remarkably good job. While the picture was not uniformly praised, it was not uniformly disparaged, either, though Murphy came in for his share of criticism.

As V. A. Musetto of the *New York Post* wrote: *"Coming to America* is best appreciated for the 'new' Murphy, although there's the danger that his abrupt change of character could backfire, leaving fans of his raunchy stuff disappointed and those previously put off by him unwilling to give him a second chance."

Robert S. Cauthorn, of the (Tucson) *Arizona Daily Star* added: "At the core of all the movie's difficulties, however, one finds that Hollywood monster [John] Landis. The director's view of comedy is shrill, his perception of humanity disfigured. The movie plays heavily on black stereotypes, but rather than being an informed parody, like Robert Townsend's *Hollywood Shuffle,* Landis puts a mean spin on the proceedings."

There was, Cauthorn admitted, a bit of humor in the picture, mostly due to Murphy's comic genius. But somehow the fact that the film was supposed to be a romantic comedy never seemed to come across clearly.

Amidst all the controversy, Arsenio Hall seemed to

stand out as one of the pluses of a film that suffered from
the mixed reviews.

Judy Winkler of the *Birmingham* (Alabama) *Post Herald* wrote: "Most of the humor comes from Hall, who steals
the show along with Lisa's nymphomaniac kid sister played
by Allison Dean."

Newsday agreed: "Director John Landis (*Animal
House, Trading Places, Three Amigos*) specializes in unrefined humor, but the broadness of the approach flattens this
particular story. Arsenio Hall makes the most of what is
basically a talent showcase. Murphy, in between unrelated
bits of business, offers constant hints of what might have
been. *Coming to America* could have been a very funny
film, but no one believed in it. And neither will you."

The *Washington Times* concurred: "An award for versatility also should go to Mr. Murphy's real-life pal, comic
Arsenio Hall, who plays Semmi, the prince's royal buddy,
as well as a fiery, obnoxious preacher, and an elderly
barber."

But Arsenio knew his place in the hierarchy of film's
production. He knew he had been invited in, and he never
tried to override the man who had asked him to get on
board.

"To me, the good sidekick knows he's not the point
guard," Arsenio said, lapsing into basketball lingo. "You
know who the leader is and why the word *co* is in front of
your name, but you also know that the *co* has got to be
there, all the same. He's not the leader, but you can't play
the game without him."

Still, the picture was a breakthrough for Arsenio. Because Eddie Murphy had chosen to take the edge off his
own high-visibility humor, Arsenio Hall had wound up not
only with the raunchier attitude, but with the best lines.

5

Room Enough for Two

The year 1988 was *the* pivotal year in the life of Arsenio Hall. He had proved himself in 1987 by becoming a symbolic draw for an entire segment of the television viewing audience in his surprise stardom as talk-show host of *The Late Show.* But instead of immediately topping that off with a big contract to continue as talk host, Arsenio did an interesting turnabout.

Instead of playing to his strength, he played to his own built-in weakness. He had always wanted to act, but he had never really succeeded at it—witness the conversation he had had with his drama teacher at Kent State. It was mostly through the influence of Eddie Murphy that he did finally decide to sign a three-picture contract with Paramount Pictures, one of which was *Coming to America.*

The question that puzzled many, of course, was the *reason* Arsenio decided not to play along with the Fox network. He *had* made good as Joan Rivers's replacement. He *had* been asked by Fox to sign for a newly refurbished *The Late Show.* Why didn't he take pen in hand and sign in?

Hall said that the "picture there" at Fox "was never

very rosy." "They weren't real nice people. At first, they made me buy my own clothes. Then they wouldn't promote me. They just didn't want to put money into something that was going to end in thirteen weeks and be replaced by *The Wilton North Report*."

He added: "Between buying my clothes and things that I needed, I just [about] broke even."

There was more. It was the *attitude* that bothered him. In Joan Rivers's autobiography, *Still Talking*, she quotes Arsenio in a story about his inadvertent meeting with Rupert Murdoch, the Australian tycoon who owned Fox:

"Never once did any [Fox] executive come to see me. In fact, I was at the Ivy restaurant in Los Angeles one night when I spotted Rupert Murdoch waiting for his car. I introduced myself, and he started fumbling through his pockets for a ticket. He thought I was with valet parking!"

"No, Mr. Murdoch," Arsenio told him. "I do your show."

To which Murdoch mumbled, "Nice to meet you."

Arsenio was also dissatisfied with his manager's advice—particularly his advice *not* to do *The Late Show* as "permanent" host. Murphy later persuaded Arsenio to drop the manager who had so little faith in him and sign up with Robert Wachs, Murphy's own manager.

Arsenio and his former manager had been in contact with King World for a projected talk show featuring Hall. King World was sympathetic to blacks; they distributed the amazingly successful *Oprah Winfrey Show*. But at the time Arsenio talked to them, a rep informed him that King World felt that America wasn't ready for two black talk-show hosts. Only one, apparently, would be acceptable to white America.

At the crucial point when Fox finally broke down and asked Arsenio to come back on board on a permanent basis to replace the disastrous *Wilton North Report*, he had signed with Wachs, and Wachs was looking away from television and toward the movies.

"Everybody was ready to give me some money. MCA. Universal. CBS. ABC. And then Paramount gave me a deal and—believe me—it wasn't the highest amount offered me. I turned down a much larger sum of money, by the millions, just to work at Paramount—because all of a sudden I realized me and my buddy"—Murphy—"could have fun under the guise of business."

When Fox came through with an offer of two million dollars to come back to them, Arsenio turned them down, reminding them: "Remember, you guys weren't very nice to me to begin with."

It was in the summer of 1988 that Arsenio Hall finally achieved the goal he had set for himself when he threw everything into his Pinto and headed for the Coast. He was signed up to appear on the Johnny Carson show—with Johnny Carson interviewing him!

Now, of course, there was a very good reason for the gig. He was promoting Eddie Murphy's *Coming to America*. Nevertheless, Hall knew that he was achieving one of the primary aims of his career.

Seated opposite his idol of so many years, he was so bemused that he gave what he later assessed as a terrible interview.

"I'm sitting there," he told Steve Pond in *Playboy* magazine, "and I'm looking at Johnny and watching him do his thing, and it was like. . . . Did you ever make love to a woman and it was real good? *Real* good? And then, years later, you're not with her, you see her and you remember how good that pussy was?

"And you think, Oh, shit, she used to put ice cubes in her mouth and. . . . And, oh, that *noise* she used to make. . . . That's what sitting at the Carson show was like."

Then, during the commercial, Carson began chatting with his guest about being a magician himself when he was a kid. After all, his research notes showed that Arsenio had been a magician.

That made Arsenio do some deep thinking. The two
of them were so much the *same*. Why not—why not—?
Somehow it all seemed *predetermined*—something that was
just *supposed* to be.

"It was the worst interview I've ever done. I was elsewhere. But I decided on the air, while doing the worst interview of my life, that I was going to do my show again."

Almost simultaneously CBS-TV made a move that
caused it all to come together for Arsenio Hall, even though
the move itself had absolutely nothing to do with him.

Not since 1972, when *The Merv Griffin Show* had been
canceled, had CBS-TV taken part in the late-night talk-
show sweepstakes. Since that time, the network had been
filling in the late hours with almost anything available. With
the Johnny Carson show chugging on its amiable way year
after year—making big bucks from advertisers of all
kinds—CBS-TV played second fiddle, just waiting. Now,
CBS decided, the time had come. The network decided
that it would try again.

What it needed was a host.

It selected Pat Sajak, a man who had become a household name since his first appearance in 1983 as the host of
the most popular show of the 1980s in America—*Wheel of
Fortune*. *Wheel* was a hit show syndicated by none other
than CBS-TV's long-departed Merv Griffin.

Sajak had started out as a weatherman on WSMV-TV
in Nashville, Tennessee, in the seventies, and had then
moved to Los Angeles to prognosticate the monotonous
weather there for KNBC-TV from 1977 to 1981. From
there he went to *Wheel,* where he became the star of the
biggest show of the year.

The announcement of Sajak's two-year contract to
play opposite *The Tonight Show (Starring Johnny Carson)*—he would be making millions—set Arsenio Hall's
blood to churning. Arsenio felt he was ready for the big
breakthrough. Being on the Carson show had revived his

interest in hosting. His competitive spirit was aroused by the news of Sajak's new project.

"I knew Sajak was going to do the Carson show [all over] again." Arsenio meant that Sajak was a carefully crafted commodity, a kind of safe-as-houses, respectable, middle-of-the-road host. If Arsenio could come up with some new wrinkle for a talk-show host, something he could make all his own, he might be able to run a kind of *race* with Sajak—and win it!

"I was watching MTV, and it dawned on me that its audience—the *kids* who see the most movies, drink the most Pepsi—did not have a talk show [modeled to their particular tastes]." And Arsenio determined that he could fill that gap as well as anyone else—*better,* in fact.

"That's when I said yes," referring not to any offer that was made to him, but to himself. Once he had made the decision, it was not long before he and Robert Wachs succeeded in heating up interest in Arsenio as a talk-show commodity.

The negotiations were tough. From the beginning Arsenio declared that he would not take the job unless he had total creative control. The traditional way to control creativity was for the star to be his own executive producer. Arsenio insisted on that.

The problem became which network to get to do the show. NBC-TV was out; it already had the top dog, Johnny Carson. CBS-TV had decided on *Wheel*'s Sajak. ABC-TV had its own successful *Nightline,* with Ted Koppel, with backup by other featured interviewers. Perhaps the Fox network would be interested?

Arsenio's reservations about Fox decided him and his manager. They went after Paramount Pictures, which had already signed Hall for exclusive rights to a number of films. Paramount could always rework its contract if it decided to produce a Hall talk show.

And so negotiations began. The first capitulation on

Paramount's part was the naming of Hall as executive producer as well as star of the program. It was harder to go along with Hall's suggestion for his producer, probably the most important executive on the show next to Hall himself.

When he had taken over *The Late Show* for Fox, Arsenio had worked with a director named Marla Kell Brown. He wanted her to act as producer for his projected show for Paramount. But since most of Arsenio's other demands—which were minor—were met and he had won over Paramount on his main point of serving as his own executive producer, he decided to let the Brown decision wait.

Eddie Murphy was elated at the successful conclusion of the main negotiations.

"When I called and told him I had been signed by Paramount, he couldn't have been happier. He kept singing 'For He's a Jolly Good Fellow,' no matter what I tried to say."

Arsenio went on thoughtfully: "There's no competitiveness between us. We share intimate secrets. We cry together. Eddie is the brother I never had."

At the time the contract was signed and the terms announced in the press, the general battle plan could have been described as targets of opportunity. With CBS going up against NBC at 11:30 P.M., there might be some viewers who would want an *alternative* to the obvious similarities between the face-to-face Sajak and Carson offerings. Why not tune in Arsenio?

The disadvantages of syndication in relation to network broadcasting usually center around an inability to establish and maintain a time slot, with the proper lead-ins in place and the segments all solidly constructed. Ironically, the advantages of syndication over network center around the mobility of the time slots—a show can be shifted at will to avoid unwanted confrontations as well as to invite desired confrontations.

For example, when Arsenio first opened in the New York market, he did not go head to head with Sajak and

Carson. Instead, he was slotted at 12:30 A.M. opposite David Letterman, then the heir apparent to Carson. Arsenio was unhappy over that, as he considered Letterman his idol. "I think Dave is state of the art. I've always said that Johnny's the longest, but Dave's the strongest." He capitulated, however, acknowledging his own needs. "I'll take anything he'll leave."

Around the rest of the country, Arsenio would debut in some places at 11:00 P.M., others at 11:30, at 10:00, in others later. It was only after a number of months of broadcasting that *The Arsenio Hall Show* settled down, to be anchored in most places opposite Johnny Carson in the 11:30 P.M. (10:30 Central Time) slot.

The three-way "race"—if there really was any—was for *cumulative* Nielsen points, not knockout blows. Sajak and Carson might be trying to pin each other to the mat, but that was in no way the strategy of Arsenio's handlers. He was an *alternative* in the late-night talk-show arena, not a win-or-lose contender. For this reason no exact scoring of blows could ever be established for Arsenio. For Sajak, it was a different story.

In preparation for the debut in 1989, Arsenio spent the balance of 1988 sharpening his delivery and developing a style for his stand-up openings. He would be playing to a more general audience than that for his current stand-ups, but he had been successful on *The Late Show* and he was confident that he could hit the right note.

"It's an uphill battle, being black, but if a black can do it—I can do it!" He told newspaper reporters that he hoped he had what he called "bicultural sensitivity to please a lot of people," and that *that* ability would allow him to be a black man doing a show not just for blacks but for everybody.

In mapping out the format for his show, Arsenio was going to make one major change that would characterize him as not just another Johnny Carson. "No desk," he said. "I'm not going to sit behind a desk and look like a businessman." He had always liked the idea of a party. "Every night is going to be a party," he said. "My guests, and the viewing audience, will be coming to my party."

Also, he wanted a smaller band than was traditional. And he wanted to let the audience play a larger role than the Johnny Carson audience did. They just came in and sat there for the show. He wanted action in front of the proscenium as well as behind it.

Paramount Pictures' marketing strategy for syndication was sound. First of all, it would try to sell the show to the largest independent station in each city. Its second choice after that would be to go to the ABC-TV network station. ABC-TV shut down at midnight, after *Nightline* aired, and then ran movies to fill the all-night schedule.

Fox was beginning to reap the whirlwind. By October, it had killed *The Late Show,* which was being aired at that time with Ross Shafer as host. A rumor spread that Paramount television was planning to advance the January debut date of the Hall show to take advantage of the gap in late-night programming. And that gave Arsenio a chance to make some news.

"I'm contractually bound to Fox not to host another talk show until January 3," he said. "And I won't. January 3 is the date my new Paramount show will debut."

And he had a chance to make a public pitch for Marla Kell Brown, his own choice for producer—a decision that had not yet been made. "There's a lot of feeling that she's too young," Arsenio said, pointing out that Brown was only twenty-seven years old. "But she helped me make a name for myself"—he meant on Fox's *The Late Show*—"and I want to go with that lady now."

On the strength of the rumors, the Fox network filed suit against Hall for signing the contract with Paramount to do his talk show. Rupert Murdoch claimed that Arsenio's deal with Paramount was a contractual violation, since Fox maintained that Arsenio agreed originally to give Fox Broadcasting first option if he ever decided to do a talk show.

The hassle was settled out of court, but *The Arsenio Hall Show* managed to garner just a little more space in the press.

By the end of the year, the strategy for both the Arsenio Hall and Pat Sajak groups had been pretty clearly drawn up. The idea was for the Sajak people to go into battle totally confident of victory and more or less unaware of any competition.

"We're not going to worry about Arsenio," said Paul Gilbert, producer of the Sajak show. It was obvious to the media that CBS-TV was not worried about anything. The network spent between four and five million dollars building a new sound stage and other facilities for the new show.

As for the Arsenio Hall group: Marla Kell Brown had been hired to produce the show at the insistence of its star. She pointed out that competition in late-night television was quite a different thing from the competition during prime-time shows. The competition there was the other networks. In late night, Brown said, "your biggest competition is the sandman."

"Hopefully there's enough room for everybody," said Frank Kelly, senior vice-president of programming at Paramount television.

"I think people place too much emphasis on the competition," Arsenio Hall said. "I'm running my own race. It's a personal best. It's me against me. I'm on after Sajak in Chicago, so I want him to do well"—in order to lead the audience in to *The Arsenio Hall Show*.

"The demographic that knows Sajak from daytime television is people who should be asleep [at 11:30]. His people are asleep. He probably would do well with a morning talk show. That's what I would have done with him if I were a CBS executive."

Even the remote opposition had something to say

about competition. "I think we'd be crazy not to care that they're out there," said Robert Morton, producer of *Late Night with David Letterman*. "But there are some shows that, when they're faced with severe competition, are in an out-and-out battle—witness the morning shows, how many different ones CBS has tried. I don't think it's that intense with the late-night shows."

Morton continued: "In fact, we've had Pat Sajak on *Letterman* talking about *The Pat Sajak Show*. There is, of course, a competitive spirit. But on the other hand, I think he'll bring another audience to late night—his daytime viewers." The ones that Arsenio had said would be asleep by that time. "That can only be helpful to late-night [scheduling]. If they like his show, maybe they'll turn to our show."

Arsenio Hall did not appear on *Letterman*. "I was booked [on the show] and then, the day of the announcement that I was going to have my own show, they canceled me. At first I wasn't upset about it, because this is war. Then I heard that Sajak was on the show. Maybe they don't consider Sajak competition," Arsenio added slyly.

Morton riposted: "We don't care about competing shows as far as booking. We have guests from the other networks all the time." Arsenio, he said, had originally been booked for a *Letterman* date, but canceled because of a schedule conflict. The only other date Hall had open was scrubbed because it fell too close to the debut date of the *Arsenio Hall Show*. "We just thought it would look a little strange to have him in one place, and then another, right away."

On the eve of the great joust, this was the way the two camps shaped up:

HOST: Pat Sajak. Caucasian male, forty-two. *Wheel of Fortune* host

NETWORK: CBS-TV

TIME: 11:30 P.M.

RUNNING TIME: 90 minutes

SIDEKICK: Dan Miller, former news anchor and Sajak's colleague back in Nashville. Was briefly anchor at Los Angeles's KCBS-TV in 1986.

STUDIO ORCHESTRA: The Tom Scott Band, all-male, jazz-rock/fusion

STYLE: Jack Paar revisited. Broad demographic appeal. Guests from show-biz superstars to politicians, authors, scientists, and men/women in the street.

PSYCHE: Conventional. At first, Sajak considered a radical move: Instead of seating guests on the right side of his desk (stage right), the way Carson did, he wanted to put guests on the left side—just to make things different. Didn't work. "I swear," Sajak admitted, "it was like looking into a mirror, we're so used to seeing it the other way. It just looked weird." But "change" was not totally out. Instead of the double-breasted suitcoats and the pocket handkerchief on *Wheel*, Sajak would wear mostly single-breasted coats without the handkerchief. Whew!

FORMAT: Desk

PROMO: Low-key, avoiding what CBS called "anticipointment"—unrealistic viewer expectations.

ADD TO SIDEKICK: Sajak considered bringing along Vanna White as sidekick from *Wheel*. But he felt good-natured ribbing between male host and female sidekick might be misconstrued: "If I'm needling some guy, it's two guys having fun. But if I'm needling a woman, I'm a cad, and if she's needling me, she's a bitch." Settled eventually on a quintessential authoritative newscaster whose towering height and Nashville accent contrasted to Sajak's elfin charm and quick wit.

And, in the other corner—

HOST: Arsenio Hall. Black male, thirty. Guest host of Fox Broadcasting's *Late Night Starring Joan Rivers.* Costar with Eddie Murphy of box-office hit *Coming to America.*

NETWORK: Syndication by Paramount Pictures.

TIME: Various.

RUNNING TIME: 60 minutes.

SIDEKICK: None.

STUDIO ORCHESTRA: Hall: "I have a sexy lady on drums; I have a sexy lady on keyboard."

STYLE: The hipness of Letterman without his cutting edge of cynicism. Star-struck fan of Hollywood glitter. Guests wide-ranging, but with younger demographic appeal.

PSYCHE: Hall: "I'm the Martin Luther King, Jr., of comedy." He plans to eliminate racism and sexism from late-night television by making sure minorities and women appear on the show. "There are a lot of people out there who don't have a talk show. I am their talk show." *The Arsenio Hall Show* will have a male announcer. "We had guys here [at Paramount] who make three hundred thou a year, saying, 'How about *The Arsenio Hall Show*?' But *Arsenio Hall After Dark* sounded sleazy. And I thought of *Arsenio,* but they said, 'You're *not* Cher.'"

FORMAT: No desk. "I just like to wing it. I'm a comedian, I come from the clubs. I know how to work an audience." Arsenio Hall will concentrate on being Arsenio. "I honestly think Joan [Rivers]'s failure was based on the fact that they tried to change Joan, they tried to tone her down. I have to be Arsenio. I'm the best Arsenio there is."

6

Coronation Night

 he debut of a new late-night talk show, according to Marvin Kitman in *Newsday,* is a historic event—the closest thing in television to a coronation. And there were two such coronations scheduled for January 1989 within a week of each other—Arsenio Hall's show slated for a Tuesday night and Pat Sajak's for the following Monday.

To Brandon Tartikoff, the TV mogul, it was no coronation—it was a very special contest between two contenders.

"This race is not a sprint," he said. "It's a marathon. Whatever burns the brightest, fades the fastest."

On debut night, there were no discernible signs of nervousness or diffidence in Arsenio Hall. He seemed marvelously free of the jitters, entirely distanced from the usual massive stage fright, and completely capable of filling the niche he had staked out for himself.

If anything, Arsenio might have been just a little too full of pep for the time of night in which he had chosen to operate. The energy level of the show was higher than that

of almost any contender for that spot. Yet such energy was
the right way to attract young viewers, the part of the population that seemed to be his primary target.

He and his staff had spent their development time
well, honing his style of stand-up, with which he opened
the show in the very same manner Johnny Carson and most
other late-night talk-show hosts opened theirs.

Because this was a debut in the big time and because
Arsenio Hall was the star of his own show and not a guest
host with nothing to prove, he and his staff carefully widened the parameters of his subject matter and the celebrities whose names he would drop. Nevertheless, in spite of
this concession to a wider audience, he did not deviate
from the general thrust of his earlier monologues, found to
be so successful on *The Late Show*. In short, he was not
eager to appear as someone other than the Arsenio Hall
whose persona was familiar to a growing number of cult
viewers.

The theory behind this "safety net" approach was that
he not bow in as a freaky other-worldly anomaly far ahead
of the general public, but as an individual in the know, instinctively a bit ahead of the crowd but not so far out front
that he might appear to be marching to a different
drummer.

> ITEM: He mixed a little sexual innuendo with current
> events. He mentioned James Brown and the fact
> that he was in jail. "He's a sex machine now," he
> remarked.
> ITEM: With his own brand of fooling around he did an
> impression of Larry Bird's basketball style.
> ITEM: Not to focus entirely on Caucasian Larry Bird,
> he did a counter routine on Magic Johnson's court
> style for the Los Angeles Lakers.
> ITEM: He said his staff had informed him of a crowd
> of hundreds outside the studio who had been un-

able to get in to the show. Most were blacks. Before his stand-up he had strolled outside to say hello to them and to thank them for coming. After a short pause, he looked into the camera and ad-libbed, in his toothy Arsenio style: "Hey! Some of those people have automatic weapons!"

By the very nature of that remark, the cool new talk-show host displayed the distinctive cutting edge that has made him popular. And yet, in spite of that element implicit in his manner, he was completely at ease and in control of any menace that might be bubbling below the surface.

These items that made up his monologue were carefully considered options that would not send shock waves into the living rooms of America. To those people who had never seen Arsenio before, his appearance itself was enough of a stimulant. The flat-top hair style, the elegant dress of a born clothes horse, the smiling, toothy, electric image—this alone could put him over.

And the strategy worked. By the time the stand-up was finished, he had reached out and touched millions via the electronic media and certainly charmed his live audience at the studio into a frenzy of jubilation and applause.

The casual viewer had not really had a chance to look over the rest of the set. At the end of the monologue the show's host strolled over to the couches for a sit-down with guest number one. Then the entire set was illuminated, the musicians scanned, and the audience panned by the cameras.

True to his promise, Arsenio had provided soft, comfortable, overstuffed couches for his guests to sit on. No desk for him, no table, nothing hard-backed or strict, just an overstuffed chair. The couches were positioned at stage right—the viewer's left as one looked at the set.

The band, composed of five musicians including Michael Wolff, the leader, was set up just to the viewer's right of center stage, with a group of special fans—the Dog Pound—to the viewer's right of them. On the Arsenio Hall set, the distance between music and conversation did not seem quite so wide as on other talk shows; there was subliminal integration between the two. Center stage was Arsenio's stand-up spot where he delivered his opening monologue and later greeted his guests.

The audience was distributed in such a way that the host could walk among the seats and engage anyone in easy conversation. Getting from one part of the set to another had been made flawlessly simple so that Arsenio could rove about whenever he felt the impulse. The cameramen simply followed him about.

The stage was glitzy bright, with green and blue predominating. One critic wrote: "It looked like some sort of show business aquarium." The decor seemed to be a fitting mirror of Hall's very slick, double-breasted, formal style of dress.

Arsenio's opening monologue for his debut was crucial to his survival. Now that he had passed that test, he moved into the second phase of his debut: the guest list.

First on was Brooke Shields, the actress and model. Arsenio led her over to the couch and seated her on the viewers' left, while he took his position in his armchair toward center stage and angled almost front-on to the cameras.

The Q & A that followed was deliberately low-profile from the start. This was no Inquisition, he seemed to be reminding everyone. His first question of Brooke Shields was: "Is it hard to be Brooke Shields?"

In a way, the question seemed almost a parody of the usual talk-show query. But of course his query had Arsenio Hall's patented edge to it. Shields had embarked on a rather difficult crusade, one to persuade young women—teenagers mostly—to remain virgins until they were married. Not an easy message to put over, given the general sociological climate of free-wheeling America.

Acting on the theory that an interviewer can ask anything if he asks it the right way, Arsenio smiled and said: "Brooke, I read somewhere that you said you were a virgin." Short pause. "How's that going?"

Shields avoided an answer, passing the question off with a smile. Obviously, she intimated, it was going very well. In which direction was not all that certain.

Then Arsenio asked Shields to explain her controversial relationship with Michael Jackson. She strolled around that question as well, evading any direct response almost effortlessly, and then Arsenio asked her what she thought about dancing.

"I can be *hot* when I'm dancing," she told him with real concern. Arsenio blinked. That was not exactly what he had in mind.

About her music, she was more forthcoming.

"I'm into a new genre called countrypolitan," she told him. "It's a crossover country and rock."

Anything else? Arsenio seemed about ready to end the interview.

"Yes. I'm pushing a new line of hair products," Shields told him, "including a crimping iron and blow dryer." She added: "It's mine."

The interview, which had verged on a diverting discussion of virginity among teenagers, had somehow steered itself away from any partisanship only to end on a commercial note, with the interviewee dutifully flogging her product. Arsenio Hall's expression of awelessness at its conclusion gave his reaction better than words ever could.

The musical break that followed Shields featured Luther Vandross, and when the number was finished, Vandross was escorted by Arsenio to the guest couch. Arsenio had made it known to his fans early on that he was an accomplished musician himself, so when he gave his opinions on music, they were expected to be those of a professional, not a fan.

"Isn't he fabulous?" Arsenio said, indicating his guest.

Vandross grinned and cringed predictably.

The musician had a weight problem. When he had made his album, he was eighty-three pounds heavier; Arsenio held up the album cover to prove the point. Now Vandross had gotten himself down to a respectable 165, and looked a whole lot better.

The two chatted knowledgeably about music in a relaxed and comfortable manner—without really uttering any earthshaking comments about musicianship in general or even in particular—after which Vandross wound up his chat with a closing remark to the audience about his affable host:

All together now: "Isn't Arsenio fabulous?"

The next guest was Leslie Nielsen, who had been parked in the greenroom during the preliminary acts. He was pushing his role of Lieutenant Drebin in the movie *Naked Gun,* certainly one of the funniest pictures of the year.

Obviously, Nielsen was the star of the first night's lineup. True to the uninhibited style of *Naked Gun,* Nielsen did a breaking wind joke that really brought down the house, then showed the device in his hand that he had used to create the sound of flatulence.

The show ended on a rather odd note. All during the monologue, the music, and the sit-down interviews, one could see a vaguely familiar face among the members of the band. It was Nancy Kulp, who had played Jane Hathaway on the 1960s sitcom *The Beverly Hillbillies.*

Finally, at the end of the show, she was introduced and after a short discussion with Arsenio Hall, the band started playing the *Beverly Hillbillies* theme song, with the audience enjoined to sing along. Everyone in the studio gave a standing ovation to the show.

With this slightly offbeat touch of nostalgia, the show ended to thunderous applause in the studio.

The ratings were unanimously up for the opener; Arsenio was rated first in New York, Chicago, Detroit, Atlanta, Sacramento, and Cleveland. There, in his birthplace, his show got a phenomenal 47 percent share of the audience when it aired at 1:00 A.M. And in New York, where he debuted opposite David Letterman at 12:30 A.M., he even beat out the old pro.

In fact, in seventeen tested markets, the show averaged a 16-percent share of the audience, a 33-percent increase over its lead-in competition and 5 share points higher than previous programming had scored in those time periods in February and November 1988. But, of course, high ratings are the normal thing for every new show. They usually drop off quickly thereafter.

The critics spotted some flaws in the production. One of these concerned the host's propensity for dropping names. For example, it was pointed out that Hall had referred to Eddie Murphy, Rob Lowe, and Cornelia Guest not in one interview—but *in one sentence!*

Another was Arsenio's habit of bowing and scraping before every guest. It was obvious that his questions should be more edged, so that the guest might be able to make a point of some kind rather than simply to swirl about in the treacly amiability of the indiscriminate host. Plugging a new movie, album, or television show was one thing; floating about in rapturous praise was nonproductive at best.

He also tended to titter nervously when a line that was supposed to get a laugh failed to do so. Instead of remarking on the density of the audience, as Carson might, he would simply giggle until moving on to the next line. He seemed habitually to avoid any kind of controversial remark, seeming always to focus on the politically correct name to attack—or drop—in effect taking the edge off his normally resolute demeanor. First-night jitters?

There were good omens as well. The host seemed to

be actually listening to the answers his guest was giving, rather than simply waiting a few moments to ask the next question on the cue card. As he sat thinking about these answers he frequently came up with some intelligent comments and sometimes brought up new questions that led the discussion into new areas.

Even in his debut show, he demonstrated the carefully nurtured ability to ad-lib. In the several times he made up his own comments on the spot, he revealed a sense of humor and fun that was just a bit barbed, but never challenging or upsetting to his mixed audience.

Best of all, the immediate connection that Arsenio made with his live audience augured well for his future in late-night TV. The smooth style he had developed, the ease with which he faced difficult situations and calmed troubled waters, and his sparkling charisma put him on a level with show-biz greats who could make it with any audience. He had a way that would allow him, as a black man, to be accepted by a white man or woman without the usual subconscious racial reservations.

The signs were there. It would be an education to see if and/or how Arsenio Hall would eliminate the negatives and accentuate the positives of his own television image.

In spite of the fact that the first show was a success, it was not quite so obvious how the ensuing nights would treat its star. By the time his main competition for the number-two slot against Johnny Carson—Pat Sajak—previewed the following Monday, where would *The Arsenio Hall Show* be?

And on the following Monday night, January 9, the question was effectively answered.

Pat Sajak entered the plush furnishings of the lavish set CBS had built for him at a cost of four million dollars plus, playing the agreed-upon role of—none other than Pat Sajak himself.

His opener was a beaut.

PAT SAJAK (glancing at his wristwatch): In less than one minute we will officially become CBS's longest-running show of the season.

Sajak then delivered a carefully written monologue with all the requisite laughs in place. He got his laughs and then engaged in a bit of chatter with the band leader, Tom Scott, in almost a carbon copy of Johnny Carson's banter with Doc Severinsen.

He then strolled over to the desk cloned from Carson's and sat down the way Carson did to chat with his guest seated on a long sofa to his right. The way Carson's guests sat, of course.

It was obvious that the jokes had been carefully constructed by a gang of gag writers who had slavishly emulated Carson's technique. And while some of them were barbed just sufficiently to get the proper kind of laugh, the Sajak delivery was so bland that the impression was that he didn't take any of the jests very seriously. Or himself either.

A very unthreatening personality.

If indeed it *was* a personality.

The Arsenio Hall Show had as its first guest Brooke Shields, a glamorous white woman, to play against the black, male, street-smart Arsenio Hall. *The Pat Sajak Show* went the opposite route. It provided the bland, low-keyed, almost improbably cool comedian Chevy Chase to play against the bland, low-keyed, almost improbably cool host Pat Sajak. The result was an amusing exchange of chatter, conceivably orchestrated by a band of gag writers beforehand, although Chase is a master at concocting his own jokes.

Because of the format of the Sajak show, guest number one slid over on the couch when guest number two arrived, and guests one and two slid over when guest number three arrived, so that guest number one was more or less a prisoner for the entire evening.

With Chase shunted aside, Joan Van Ark—one of the regulars on the nighttime soap opera *Knots Landing*—became guest number two. Sajak and she got to talking about her role as hostess of various parades and beauty pageants, often teamed with Bob Barker.

PAT SAJAK: Tell him that last batch of Grecian Formula is not working well.

Guest number three was a twosome, actually guests three and four, The Judds, a mother and daughter team who had a CBS prime-time special of their own. They sang a song and chatted for a while. In fact, the daughter got glummer and glummer as her mother forged cheerfully ahead.

After guests three and four were shunted aside, on came Peter V. Ueberroth, number five, the departing commissioner of baseball. He told Sajak that he was in favor of continuing to sell beer at baseball games and that he was against the use of drug testing to check up on his players.

It was at that point that Chevy Chase raised his hand to attract Pat Sajak's attention.

PAT SAJAK: Yes?
CHEVY CHASE: Could I be excused to go to the bathroom, sir?

And so it went.

As John J. O'Connor of *The New York Times* wrote: "Physically, Mr. Sajak is almost eerily ordinary. His haircut suggests Yale 1958. From certain angles, he resembles Frank Gorshin doing an impression of Dan Quayle. He is, in short, a very comfortable sort of fellow, holding in reserve the right to be terribly wicked."

The New York Times compared the shows: "One show is affably low-key, in the mode of Johnny Carson and easy-listening radio. The other program is glitzy, aggressively friendly, hyperkinetic. Take your choice."

And, by way of explanation:

"Where the Sajak show virtually ignores the studio audience, Mr. Hall revels in getting the crowd worked up. They cheer, they scream, they hold up banners saying, 'We Love You, Arsenio.' The cameras are constantly panning the studio bleachers where the fans are jumping up and down with joy."

It was difficult to say if anyone had managed to win the first round. Perhaps it was David Letterman, after all.

When Letterman opened opposite Arsenio Hall in New York, he made no mention of his competition on his Tuesday night show.

However, in a sly bit of inside humor, his bandleader, Paul Shaffer, made mention of the fact that David Letterman's show was "the number-one talk show party in America."

The phrase was lifted intact from a commercial Arsenio Hall's syndicate had used in advertising *his* show. The audience got the gag.

They stood and applauded.

7

The Palace Guard

Within the first week of airing, *The Arsenio Hall Show* proved that it had not only an inbuilt initial excitement, but also an inherent ability to survive the ratings battle. The initial viewing figures told the story.

When the show premiered, it hit a 3.4 rating the first night, with each rating point representing 921,000 households tuned in to the show, and, although the numbers tailed off a bit the rest of the week, they were consistently high.

"We promised a rating in the high 2s," Arsenio said about the original estimates, "and started out with a 3.4 the first week."

After the initial first-week broadcasts, the ratings figures did drop a bit, but by the end of the month they had returned and firmed up at a 3-plus level. The numbers continued strong in February and by March the show was an acclaimed success.

Certain of the guests helped skyrocket the numbers, of course. When Arsenio persuaded his good friend Eddie

Murphy to appear, the ratings in Washington, D.C., showed that almost a million people were watching in that area alone.

What was more, *The Arsenio Hall Show* was being seen in 92 percent of the country on 135 different television stations. The crossover concept that had so worried the television moguls at Paramount had worked inconceivably well *for* Arsenio Hall, not against him. He was obviously considered as much a television icon by whites as by blacks.

Now the question: How had this young upstart done it? How had he been able to gain so many followers in the white as well as the black population? How had he been able to garner such support in so highly competitive a broadcasting area? And against such formidable competition?

To Arsenio Hall, there was a very simple answer. "I tried to do something different." He went back to previous television history for a comparison. "Alan Thicke couldn't take Johnny Carson. I'm young and black. If a guy's watching Johnny Carson, I want his kids in the other room to be watching me."

He had never had it in mind to do in Carson. He was concerned mostly with *establishing* Arsenio Hall with a younger, more hip audience.

"The idea," he elaborated, "is to fill a void. I know the MTV crowd does not have a talk show. It's been a big party for me. The ratings are higher than anticipated. I'm in shock. Even white people are watching."

One point that was not lost on any television executive who might have been looking for answers to the phenomenon of Arsenio Hall as *the* talk-show host of 1989 was the key fact that the star was an entity unto himself—a *real* person.

It might be easier to explain what Arsenio Hall *was* by pointing out what he was *not*.

ITEM: He was *not* a pseudo-persona created by committee.

ITEM: He was *not* a concoction fabricated from a definitive list of qualities associated with superstar formulation.

ITEM: He was *not* a prefabricated collage stuck together with Scotch tape and rubber cement for the delectation of the dilettante viewer.

Arsenio Hall was the individual who had been personally involved in every key selection made in building the creative machine that put him on the air.

He was the executive producer of his own program, an executive producer who did not sit back in an office and read *The Wall Street Journal* and *Variety,* but who rolled up his sleeves and got down to the business of interfacing, analyzing, and communicating with the people he had hired to work for him.

Arsenio Hall was his own talent scout, selecting not only the staff that surrounded him, but considering every day the people he wanted to invite as guests on his show.

Everything about *The Arsenio Hall Show* had his stamp firmly implanted on it—engraved with his own personal flourish.

A look at one element of the show demonstrates how Arsenio individualizes everything he does. He had hand-picked the musical group that backed the show. He had spent weeks traveling from coast to coast hunting for its proper composition. He had not been satisfied simply to hire a leader and give the leader carte blanche to choose his own sidemen.

For example, Arsenio had selected the bassist, John B. Williams, on his own. Williams had had experience playing with Doc Severinsen on the Johnny Carson show. He had found the original drummer, Terri Lyne Carrington, doing a people-are-talking type of show in New York City.

The musical director and keyboardist, Michael Wolff, had played on the Johnny Carson show. Arsenio had met him ten years ago and knew his work well. Wolff was an integral part of the total 1989 *Arsenio Hall Show*.

In the weird and wonderful world of late-night talk, the personality and talents of the bandleader can never be overstressed. Technically, the second banana of the Johnny Carson show was Ed McMahon, the affable sidekick who always sat to the left of the screen and chuckled loudly at every good gag the boss produced—and some bad ones, too.

At times, however, when the monologue buckled at the seams and tumbled into the pits, it was the *third* banana to whom Carson turned, glancing off sharply to his left—the viewer's right—to catch a glimpse of Doc Severinsen, the epitome of sartorial bad taste, for a sight gag or a voice-over comment or whatever he might come up with.

Arsenio had opted *not* to have a second banana to laugh at his jokes and cackle at his extravagances, so the music director had to serve as number-two banana. And Arsenio knew that this one had to have perfect rapport with him.

Certainly he agonized over the selection of his musical director. The expected move would be to hire a black superstar. But Arsenio was sensitive to the imbalance of having two black personalities always on camera. In the end he decided he would have to go with someone white.

Michael Wolff had been a jazz player for years, playing piano with jazz vibist Cal Tjader and later with saxophonist Cannonball Adderley. Between 1972 and 1979, he had played in bands led by Sonny Rollins, Airto and Flora Purim, and in the Thad Jones–Mel Lewis Jazz Orchestra. In 1979 Wolff finally got an offer to become conductor and piano accompanist for jazz singer Nancy Wilson. And that led to his meeting one day in 1979 with a young comedian named Arsenio Hall.

Wolff remembered that day vividly. "I was with Nancy Wilson, along with John B. [Williams] and Roy McCurdy, playing in Chicago when a young comedian named Arsenio Hall was called in to replace the comic who was already scheduled." Wolff smiled. "We helped him relax."

Arsenio remembered that day as well. "Michael [Wolff] and John B. [Williams]—they were just very good to the new kid who was nervous, who had just been told that Nancy's manager was flying [in from Los Angeles] to see him," Arsenio said, pausing to reflect. "In this business, people just don't take the time to be nice. Not to opening acts who need to use your dressing room, so to have somebody be nice, you *remember* it. I always said if I ever make it, I want to go back and grab those guys."

He and Wolff hit it off immediately, even though Arsenio instantly came up with criticism of Wolff's leadership abilities.

"You are one of the best musicians I ever heard," he told him, "but you're kind of lax as a conductor."

Wolff didn't like the comment but could think of no quick riposte.

Arsenio continued. "You kind of let things slide. You need to be a little tougher."

Wolff apparently took the criticism to heart. "I thought [what Arsenio said] was pretty cool."

Arsenio kept telling Wolff that he had aspirations to become a talk-show host. "When I get my own talk show," he told Wolff, "you're going to be the bandleader and musical director."

Wolff said, "Sure, man." Truth was, "I really didn't think he'd make it," Wolff confessed. "I never paid much attention to him [in those days]."

Not only did Arsenio make it to the big time, but he kept his promise to Wolff and went to him immediately to front for his new show's band.

"It's the greatest thing that has ever happened to me,"

said Wolff. "Well, the second greatest thing." A pause. "Actually, this is *better* than the first time I got laid."

Arsenio was able to use Wolff not only as the musical director, but as a comic second banana as well. Wolff, like Arsenio, had always really wanted to be a comic. In New York, he had taken improv workshops with Second City veteran Marty Friedman and had studied acting at the Herbert Berghoff Studios. During their days with Nancy Wilson, Hall and Wolff often worked out comic lines. One of the first exchanges between the two on *The Arsenio Hall Show* was the following:

> ARSENIO HALL: I didn't know you were from down South.
> MICHAEL WOLFF: Yeah. I grew up in Mississippi.
> ARSENIO: Mississippi? That's deep.
> WOLFF: Yeah. I grew up Jewish in the South. We didn't know *who* to hate.

Arsenio had left the "voice" of the band more or less up to Wolff, but he had picked most of the musicians himself.

At the time the show premiered, it was a five-piece group: Wolff's keyboard; Starr Parodi, second keyboard; John B. Williams, bass; Peter Maunu, guitar; and Terri Lyne Carrington, drums. Carrington was replaced by Chuck Morris in May 1989.

Wolff based his sound on the jazz concept developed by Miles Davis. "He's my hero," Wolff admitted. "I am a jazz guy first of all. My experience has always been playing with black people. That's the influence that has been the most important for me. That's why Arsenio and I get along so well. I know what he likes, more or less, and that's what I like. He loves jazz. So we sneak it in. What I feel happy about is to be a jazz guy and be on TV and be able to impart, however subliminally, some of that culture and some of those values. If you're going to be commercial, it's not a bad way to go."

Wolff liked to mix up Motown, rhythm and blues, and rock in his selections, centered on his acoustical piano. In his arrangements, he let each of the players go to his or her strengths. He also followed Arsenio's basic concept for the show in never trying to be anyone other than himself. While Doc Severinsen tried to outdo himself every night in dressing outlandishly, Wolff from the beginning appeared always as Michael Wolff, the rumpled, unshaven keyboardist.

Wolff's garb had nothing to do with getting out of the shadow of Carson's third banana. It had to do with Arsenio Hall's penchant for clothing. Arsenio wanted to have the freedom of dressing to the nines or appearing in whatever special fashion he wanted whenever he wanted. Wolff's appearance, as if he had slept all night in his car, was perfect to set off Hall's exceptionally hip taste.

Wolff's personality allowed Arsenio to make excellent use of him on the show. He was the perfect foil, Arsenio felt, for Chuck Woolery, host of *The Love Connection,* when they did a gag version of the dating show early in 1989. Three women came down from the audience to play the game, with Wolff as the available man.

"I actually went on the date, on the night of the Oscars, then came back and talked about it on the show," Wolff said. "We went to Pink's and had a chili dog, then to the Improv, but nobody was there because of the Oscars. Then we went to Lucy's Tacos, and we had to eat in the car with the motor running because there was something wrong with my car. Then when I took her home, she couldn't find her keys, so I had to help her break into her apartment. It was like a twelve-minute segment, and it got a lot of laughs."

Another time Arsenio, on the spur of the moment, told Wolff to break a date to see the movie *Lethal Weapon* in order to take out a sixty-year-old mother of five who was sitting in the studio audience.

"She was the sweetest thing," Wolff said, "so I jumped off the stage and gave her a hug, and she came over and sat at the piano. That was embarrassing, but it was fun. Of course we did not go to the movies together."

Wolff's primary accolade for his second-banana job came from *Playgirl* magazine; the editors selected him as one of the Sexiest Men of the Year 1989!

As for Wolff himself, he sums up his job on the show in these words: "Arsenio hired me to be me."

The members of the behind-the-scenes staff had as much to do with the success of the show as those up front. The key figure behind the scenes was Marla Kell Brown, the producer of the show.

"I've always really felt that I thrive on chaos," she said, talking about her work in network television. "I think that the places where I've done the best have been the most chaotic. *The Late Show* is a perfect example of that. It was a difficult place. And a very bitter time on the show, because after Joan Rivers left, it was a mess.

"But I liked the opportunity of meeting all the new hosts, whereas everybody else was so frustrated that there wasn't one permanent host. And there was a lot of resentment among the staff about who was coming in to take over.

"I was Arsenio's first choice for producer for his new show, but I wasn't Paramount's. I think it was because I'm young and they were launching a whole new show with a host that really hadn't had a lot of experience. And they had never met me. If I was in their shoes, I think I may have had some concerns, too."

Nevertheless, the chemistry between star and producer was perfect. They made a good team.

"We really provide a great balance for each other," Brown said. "I think because I come from a suburban environment"—Wilmette, near Chicago—"I'm able to say [to Hall] things like, 'I don't understand that reference.' Part of it's also because I'm white; part of it's because I'm a woman."

Arsenio's comment was usually: "Marla, you are so sheltered."

Brown's might be: "Hey, I grew up on *The Brady Bunch*; there are a lot of people out there that know that."

When Brown was finally allowed an interview with the Paramount executives, they were very direct with her.

"Do you really think you can handle the pressure?" they asked. "We're going to call you up, we're going to be screaming at you. Do you think you're ready for this?"

MARLA KELL BROWN: Oh, yeah, yeah.

In the weeks before the show premiered, Brown had a great deal to do with setting its tone and pace.

"Working with Arsenio is very easy," she said. "He's very comfortable working with women. He grew up with women. His grandmother, mother, godmother raised him. A lot of men may not like to be supervised by women, but Arsenio's very comfortable that way."

Brown's interest was always in putting Arsenio Hall over as he wanted to be put over.

"I'm very aware that this is *The Arsenio Hall Show*," she said. "I don't have such an ego that I have to put my mark on it more than it is. Some people would say that's a female trait. I'm not sure, but our director—who is also a woman—wants to make *him* look great. If there's a shot that doesn't make him look great, she's not going to want to take it. And I only want guests on that are really going to make him look good."

Brown had developed a working style that was open and informal.

"I think people have the feeling that they can say anything to me. We throw around a lot of ideas. If something goes wrong, I want to find out why, but I don't get off on announcing in a meeting how someone screwed up. I never yell. That isn't a relief that I get, which I think is very unusual.

"Very often there's a lot of yelling, slamming of doors on shows like these. Arsenio's not like that, either. We're a very even-keel kind of place. And we have a lot of fun. I don't really think of it as a job. It's just my way of life."

But the work is a full-time job, without any question.

"I work from about nine A.M. to nine P.M. and then at night between eleven P.M. and one A.M. I'm on the phone with Arsenio, watching all the different shows, talking about the next day's show. You have to love it, because it's just so constant.

"I can't watch television without thinking of who I should be booking. I can't read newspapers, see a magazine, without thinking about the show."

8

Up to Speed

For five hours Andrea Johnston stood in a long line outside Stage 29 on the Paramount lot where Arsenio Hall performed his five-nights-a-week late-night television talk show. A *Newsweek* stringer sought out the seventeen-year-old among dozens of other teenagers in the line and discovered that she was a visitor to Los Angeles.

What was she doing wasting her time standing in line for a talk show?

"I'm waiting to see Arsenio Hall in person."

The stringer was surprised. Teens and trend-setters are the most elusive of all television viewers. They spend money on everything and for years advertisers have been trying to find some sure-fire method to reach them. As far as the demographics showed, they did not watch talk shows—presumably because chit-chat reminded them too much of school.

When Andrea was confronted with that data she just shook her head. It was not that teenagers did not like talk shows. It was that they had seen most of them—once. "The

94

other [talk shows]," she said, "they're too boring. *This* is more us."

By the summer of 1989 Arsenio Hall was attracting 1.9 million viewers under the age of thirty-four, which was 200,000 more of that segment of society than David Letterman was drawing, and 800,000 more than Pat Sajak.

Arsenio had worked his way up to number two, just behind Johnny Carson. Advertisers were aware of the importance of those telling figures. Amazingly, a black man had succeeded in attracting the most elusive of all audiences, composed of blacks *and* whites *and* every other shade. How had he been able to cross over?

"To be successful as a black man in this country," Hall said, "you have to be bicultural. White people can function in a white world and only concern themselves with white things. But a black man has to know it *all*."

He explained, "I have to be able to understand the ins and outs of Dan Quayle's political life and also understand why James Brown's in jail." Pause. "But not Johnny. He isn't *expected* to know who wrote 'My Girl' or even what's going on with Nelson and Winnie Mandela. All he has to do is to be funny about John Tower."

Arsenio knew instinctively that his color *added* to the weight of his audience's expectations. From the start he had known that he would have to exploit that potential. And he apparently had found the secret of doing it.

Not all the assessments of Arsenio Hall as a talk-show host were positive. There was a generally accepted notion that he was much too adoring of his big-name guests. His attitude of subservience to them annoyed many viewers. More than one critic faulted him for immaturity and inexperience at his craft.

And that inexperience sometimes got him into trouble. One night, for example, when he was interviewing Sheena Easton, he let slip a tasteless sexist slur. Easton did not let it pass. She was outraged and told her host so in no uncertain terms. Arsenio blinked, shook his head, admitted he had put his foot in his mouth, and held his head in chagrin.

But most of the time his chats with celebrities were minus the mortification of slips of the tongue. By now he had begun to take part actively with many of his musical guests. For example, when he booked The Temptations he joined in with them in a rendition of "My Girl," and smoothly mimicked their bodily gestures as they worked the number.

Arsenio continued to work on his attitude toward celebrities and superstars. He had never really managed to treat them without overblown deference or a kind of wary diffidence. He was still trying to find the secret of proper rapport with such people. The key to his show was that it was a "fun party." How to fit in superstars with just plain Janes and Joes continued to elude him.

He himself once tried to explain the problem. "Some people would have asked Melissa Gilbert about Rob Lowe."

The actress, formerly of the television series *Little House on the Prairie,* a one-time girlfriend of Rob Lowe, had initiated a paternity suit against Lowe. Not only that, but Melissa's sister was playing one of Roseanne Barr's daughters on the troubled *Roseanne* show. Arsenio could have pursued the paternity suit *and* gone after her about her sister's view of the problems on the *Roseanne* set.

Instead, he asked her simply: "What's your baby like?" and, "What kind of pregnant mom are you?"

In the end, Melissa Gilbert wrote: "Arsenio—you give good interview."

"I didn't [ask her the obvious]," Arsenio explained. "I knew that would make her uncomfortable. I'm inviting her to my house. And as long as the [ratings] numbers remain as they are, I've got a feeling the people want me to continue to do what I'm doing.

"It's not an *interview* for me. I have *conversations* with the stars. I want to just relax and have fun and have a good time. When I'm talking to Sammy Davis, Jr., there is a respect that this man paved a road I am walking on. You see, I'm this bicultural comic animal who has things to say about Estelle Getty, but I also have things to say about La Toya Jackson. There is a respect for my elders and all those little things I have been taught."

Because Arsenio had always thought of his talk show as a party, he felt the need to be careful in his selection of a wardrobe. In his youth he had been intrigued by the elegance of Johnny Carson's getup every night.

Carson, being slight and so easy to drape, had the right build for clothes. His success as a clotheshorse had eventually spawned a designer brand of men's clothing named after him.

What Arsenio Hall engineered for his look was a combination of formal and informal—a kind of eclectic hodgepodge that delighted his fans but could certainly prove disconcerting to a staid fashion analyst. For example, one night he might appear in a double-breasted Italian silk suit, wearing a ruby stud in his left earlobe. This kind of costume was standard during his early months onstage.

But as he eased into the role, he appeared occasionally in totally informal outfits—sometimes rigs resembling Indian button-down long-waisted jackets. One night he came out in a black leather biker's uniform. And so he might Ping-Pong from intensely formal to ultra-informal.

However, no matter what kind of clothes he wore, he was always impeccably assembled. He, like Carson, was an excellent clotheshorse. And, somehow, no matter how outrageous the clothing or how dazzling the color, he carried the attire like a professional model.

His talent for fashion paid off handsomely in a public relations sense as well. In October 1991 Arsenio was selected by Mr. Blackwell as the top male of the Best Dressed entertainers on television.

"From jazzy jackets to snazzy suits, Hall mixes classic, contemporary, and cutting-edge fashions with equal ease," Blackwell wrote in *TV Guide*. He tabbed Arsenio as a "Sultan of Style."

The original concept of his talk show, as Arsenio had long ago conceived it, included having fun in a more or less *unrehearsed* way. That urge to spontaneity carried its own built-in time bomb. When any entertainment is open-ended enough to function in an impromptu fashion there are going to be problems. And from the beginning it was decided that there would be none of those fake ad-libs—typical pre-fabricated "snappers" that are funny responses to pre-scripted comments by guests.

"Do that," commented producer Brown, "and you take away what's magical about [Arsenio] Hall. He has a little-boy quality that makes him special. But it also makes him seem a little raw."

But raw didn't really matter to his fans—nor to his guests. In fact, Arsenio had prepared a so-called Wall of Fame backstage at Paramount Pictures. On the wall were hung white placards with huge scribblings on them—written by guests and signed with their names.

KIRSTIE ALLEY: You are really hot. Oh, baby, baby. Ooooo!

JAMIE LEE CURTIS (two wide-mouthed lipstick impressions followed by): Do you know what this means?

BO JACKSON: Hey, trapezoid head! Your show is kicking ass and I love it!

JAMES CAAN: Thanks, it was fun, but the sunglasses hurt a little bit.

KATHLEEN TURNER: Arsenio, I think I like you.

LOU DIAMOND PHILLIPS: Arsenio, I fought to get you the role as my brother in *Young Guns II,* but they said your hair wasn't long enough and that I didn't

have as many teeth as you. Oh well, maybe we'll
do *Twins II*.

As the season progressed, the show's format was coa-
lescing. One critic who was doing an update at the end of
the first year noted that it was "more like a revival meeting
than a TV talk show."

There was good reason for the critic to use that term.
An effort was made before each show to infuse that spirit
of an old-fashioned revival meeting into the audience. That
spirit was pumped up beforehand by two people unseen by
the television viewers: Daily Pike and Burton Richardson.

Daily Pike did for Arsenio Hall what Arsenio had
done for years for singing stars and comics who were headline attractions when he was their warm-up man.

Each night Pike would appear in front of the crowd
exactly where Arsenio Hall would stand later on.

"It's official!" he would shout. "Welcome to *The Arsenio Hall Show!*"

Pike had as much intensity and energy as Arsenio himself. He usually came out before the seated crowd twenty
minutes prior to taping time. Taping time was usually in
the afternoon; air time was late night, of course.

"We want to bond as an audience," Pike would say in
his loud-mouthed, drill-instructor voice.

"Hey! Turn to the person on your left." People in the
audience would do that, slightly amused, slightly self-conscious. "Right!" Pike would shout. "Now, put a hand on
their shoulder!" The audience would follow instructions,
losing a little of their self-consciousness. "Now give them
a big hug." And hug they did—all of them.

Then Pike would begin to work his way through the
crowd, wade right out into it, talking to visitors from Ar-
kansas or Maine or wherever, chatting them up about their
hometowns or telling jokes.

After a quarter of an hour of this, he would turn the

preshow, pep-rally dial up another notch or two by introducing, for the first time, Arsenio Hall's famous announcer, Burton Richardson!

And Burton Richardson would come out, bow, and accept the volleys of applause.

"Now!" Pike would shout. "Now, we're going to practice clapping."

Generally at this juncture, everyone would be turned on enough to begin clapping spontaneously.

"More clapping!" Pike would shout. There would be more.

Then Pike would announce that Richardson was going to do his famous voice-over signature—the intro that would bring out Arsenio Hall.

More applause.

It was Richardson's turn to run through his socko signature:

"From Stage Twenty-nine, on the planet we call Earth, it's Arsennnnnnnioooooooooo Hallllll!"

Yah! Hurrah! Cheers! Woof, woof, woof! Scream, scream, scream.

In the midst of the screaming and the barking, Michael Wolff and his musicians would be introduced by the now hyperkinetic Daily Pike, with each individual receiving a screaming ovation.

At this point Wolff and his gang would do a cranked-up version of a riff, which would once again pump up the volume.

"Remember!" Pike would suddenly yell. "When Arsenio appears, I want you to erupt! Eeeeee-rupt! Like a volcano! A volcano!"

Screaming, cheering, yelling, barking—

The stage lights would begin flashing off and on. The barking would become deafening. Abruptly, Arsenio Hall would appear in the center, silent, bowed, waiting.

The show was on!

Arsenio did his preliminary piece of business—rushing across to salute Michael Wolff, his second banana, with the traditional sign: extended forefinger touching Wolff's extended forefinger. The reminder by his father always to be number one.

Then came the second traditional move: the reference to the section of the stage just to the right (stage left) of the band—the famous Dog Pound. The space was reserved for special guests of all kinds. When Arsenio announced the Dog Pound, he would always refer to its members as "Those are the people who . . ." and then proceed to lay down a comic one-line definition for the evening.

Once the Dog Pound was introduced, the cameras would pan over the group, showing them waving and shouting. But their movements soon became a ritual. All the people in the Dog Pound would crank their right arms around in circles and bark like dogs.

"Woof, woof, woof!" or "Roof, roof, roof!"

This "woof woof" Arsenio Hall show rite caused an amusing exchange of print talk in the more elite publications of America.

It started in a paragraph in the November 13, 1989, issue of *Time* magazine, bylined by Richard Zoglin, describing the Dog Pound segment of the Arsenio Hall show:

Hall raises a clenched fist and rotates it in a circle, inspiring the crowd to respond with its trademark barking chant: "Wooh! Wooh! Wooh!"

To which the ponderous and stately *New Republic* magazine responded in its December 25, 1989, issue:

Time's November 13 cover story on Arsenio Hall was a minor classic in the art of not getting it. . . . Even many middle-aged white magazine editors know that the chant is "Roof! Roof! Roof!"—a detail that escaped not only *Time*'s editors, but its vaunted fact-checking department. . . . C'mon *Time*, let's get busy.

In response to *that*, *Time*'s Christopher Porterfield, who edited the story for *Time*, wrote to the *New Republic*:

I hope *The New Republic*, so far out front on black idioms, will enlighten us all as to why "Roof!" is hipper than "Wooh!"

That was *not* the end of the exchange. The *New Republic* continued with the following:

Washington Post columnist Richard Cohen instructs us that the audience chant Arsenio leads is neither "Wooh! Wooh! Wooh!" as *Time* had it, nor "Roof! Roof! Roof!" as we corrected it, but "Woof! Woof! Woof!" Cohen confirmed this with a spokesman for Arsenio, who told him that the cheer derives from Hall's hometown of Cleveland, where Browns' football fans sitting in the section of cheap seats known as the "dog pound" woof to express support for the team. Of course, whatever Arsenio says about this goes. But in our own defense, we'd like to note that the sound he makes is a dog's bark, variously transliterated in English as arf, woof, roof, or ruff. Take your pick. But whatever noise dogs make, they do not go wooh! wooh! except possibly at the offices of *Time*. We stand partially corrected.

With the increasing popularity of *The Arsenio Hall Show* through 1989, the names of the guests escalated in their recognition factor. Eddie Murphy had been one of the big names from the start, but now Mike Tyson might drop by just to chat with Hall. In fact, at one time Michael Jackson did a walk-on. Even the usually non-talk-show guest Robert De Niro appeared one night.

One of the unexpected bonuses was that Janet Jackson, who was just launching her Rhythm Nation world tour, appeared on the show unannounced—something that would have been unheard of when the show first started. It was part of Hall's ability now to provide an occasional surprise guest for his growing audience.

And, "Jack Nicholson knows De Niro has been on the show, De Niro knows that the people he hangs out with in New York watch it," Kim Swann, then Arsenio Hall's talent executive, pointed out. "These people talk, and they do watch TV."

Swann (now vice president of Arsenio Hall Communications) was in charge of locating guests for the show. She had a staff of three people working for her, and received many videocassettes from hopefuls who wanted to appear.

"I may not watch everything," she confessed, "but I do watch a good amount of it. My favorite thing is to watch a new show [on TV] before it airs and be able to spot the breakout character [for us to have on ours]."

Her goal, always, was to set up special moments on the program, such as "when Jesse Jackson walks out and receives a standing ovation. Or when Sugar Ray Leonard and Muhammad Ali appear on stage, unannounced."

Arsenio Hall attributes his success at least partially to his interest in and nurture of the disenfranchised. He always considered it a duty to book black performers who were rarely showcased on television. He felt it his duty to establish a minority internship program at his production company. And he wanted his audience to reflect his own multicultural outlook on life.

He still considered himself the luckiest man in this universe to be doing what he was doing for a living—and a good one, at that!

"I was born to do this. When I'm in the spotlight, I'm gone. I love it more than anything in the world. When everyone is barking and screaming, it's the best feeling I've ever felt, like a three-point jumper with one second left in the championship game against Boston. Better than an orgasm."

One night as he looked out into his audience, it suddenly struck him full force. "Out there I saw Mexican kids and black kids and white kids," he said. "And I thought, there's a message here. Nobody [out there]'s doing coke. Nobody's wearing gang colors. These kids are just having a good time. Over me. Imagine—*me*—having that kind of power."

It was an emotional rush that Johnny Carson or David Letterman could never have experienced.

"The show has to turn on my soul as a black man," Arsenio said. So there is always a black guest on the program, and musicians outside the mainstream—like female rap artist MC Lyte.

"I think I created something for a group that didn't have a show," Arsenio said. "There's so much Bobby Brown. New Kids on the Block. Melissa Etheridge. Kids identify with artists on a daily basis who are just stars and have never been on a show."

Arsenio did not like to be called the world's hippest man.

"Hey, if I was the hippest man in the world, the show would have problems. Even things that are hip in me I have to pull back on. I get letters from people who say, 'I watch the show because it helps me understand what my kids like and it keeps me young.' I use terminology sometimes that I have to explain for my audience because I've now found that my demographics are spreading out. I'm not the hippest man in the world because my Aunt Maggie who works in a hospital in Cleveland watches the show and understands it."

Arsenio Hall would never want to be the new Johnny Carson. He would never be mainstream enough for that. And there was no surefire indication of how long he was going to last in the slot he had created for himself, either.

But he had fans and plenty of them. To a lot of them, he was exactly what Wayne Gretzky, the California-based, transplanted Canadian ice-hockey star, wrote on the placard backstage when he appeared on the show:

"To Arsenio—Thanks for a great. You are the best."

9

The Madonna Show

It had to happen. *The Arsenio Hall Show* was bound to score one brilliant coup in its first year and a half of syndication.

That coup occurred on May 1, 1990, when Madonna visited Arsenio Hall.

Not only did the Madonna show put him on the map demographically for millions of viewers who had never even heard of him, but it drew in all the viewers possible in the range where he attracted most of his audience—the eighteen to thirty-five age group.

The show earned a 6.5 rating, which meant that almost six million households were tuned in to hear what Madonna said to Arsenio and what Arsenio said to Madonna. The total of six million households (the actual figure was 5,986,500) represents an average of four people per household—meaning that twenty-four million people were wired in to *The Arsenio Hall Show* that night!

Madonna is one of those amazing comets that streaks across the entertainment heavens. Like Cher, she was always known by one name. Born in 1959 in Bay City, Michi-

106

gan, she is a contemporary of Arsenio Hall. When she was very young the family moved to Pontiac, Michigan, where her father worked for General Motors. The neighborhood was black and white. Madonna's friends were mostly black. Dropping out of the University of Michigan, she moved to New York, joined a dance school, and learned to discipline herself. Soon she was singing as well as dancing, and then writing songs as well as singing them.

The struggle upward was hard, but so was Madonna. She was beginning to get bookings in some of the sleazy nightclubs in Manhattan when her first album was released—*Madonna,* in 1983. The second, *Like a Virgin,* appeared in 1984. That was enough to get her noticed. And by being noticed, she got her next big break: a part in the movie *Desperately Seeking Susan,* released in 1985. In it she played someone who was almost exactly her twin. That image caught the public fancy. Some of her songs were used in the film.

Carried along on a crest of publicity by the movie, she released her third album, *True Blue,* in 1986, *Who's That Girl?* in 1987, and *Like a Prayer* in 1989. Cutting across the albums were her first MTV videos. She was a smash in them: Her electric personality, her good looks, her muscular coordination, her sexual attraction made them blockbusters.

But Madonna knew, in the words of the strippers in *Gypsy,* that she had to have a gimmick. Her gimmick was to shock with gestures, implications, specifics. As soon as she shocked, the shockee responded: tasteless. But, on second thought, what *was* tastelessness unless it was a judgmental assessment? And so she shocked, persisted, and conquered.

The details of Madonna's life were the stuff of which gossip copy was made. Everybody knew intimately all about her struggles, her triumphs, her tragedies, her interludes of desperate overwork.

This icon of tastelessness—where could she go to publicize her latest movie role? She had been cast as Breathless
Mahoney in Warren Beatty's *Dick Tracy.* Of course the
two stars were rumored to be having an affair. Where could
she discuss this in public?

Not on the Carson show. Not on the Letterman show.
Not on the Sajak show. Not even on the Morton Downey,
Jr., show. *The Arsenio Hall Show* was the inevitable se-
lection.

From the beginning, Arsenio's Madonna show was an
eclectic mix of surprise, shock, and serendipity. When the
band finished its initial lead-in and the announcer bawled
over the catcalls, woof-woofs, and screams, "Here's Arsenio!" the curtains parted and—surprise!—it was Madonna
who appeared.

She was dressed as she had been many times before in
superwhite. Her hair was bleached blond once again; she
had long practiced the habit of switching arbitrarily from
blond to brunette simply to keep her audiences in suspense
over what color to expect.

"Madonna exuded a look that said half high-class, half
street tramp." That was Bob Remington, of the *Edmonton
Journal,* on her overall appearance.

When Arsenio appeared shortly afterward, it turned
out that—surprise again!—he was dressed in coordinated
black. Black for black; white for white.

As the two stars stood there trying to get the shouting
quieted down, Arsenio grinned his toothy grin. "If I'm going to be chumped, I might as well be chumped by the
best," he said as he watched Madonna sashaying through
the audience in her matching white jacket and pants.
Around her neck was a gold-link chain with a heavy medal-
lion in the shape of a dollar sign.

Finally the cheering and stomping subsided and the
talking began.

It was obvious immediately that Madonna was enjoying herself hugely. At first she and Arsenio kidded around with Michael Wolff and several of the musicians in a deliberate game of misnaming one another, an unscripted routine that wound up when Arsenio finally got down to the serious business of questioning Madonna about her life, her loves, and her celebrity.

He started out pursuing a current theme.

"We like your new video," he told her, referring to "I'm Breathless: Music from and Inspired by the Film *Dick Tracy*"—probably one of the longest titles in video history.

Everybody cheered.

Arsenio then proceeded to the nitty-gritty. He asked Madonna about a line in her new "Vogue" song on the video. It was a line about Rita Hayworth giving "good face." What did that mean? he asked her.

There were squeals and yowls of anticipation.

Madonna smiled. "It's not exactly like giving good BLEEP," she said.

More cheers and screams.

The two of them then indulged in a bit of give-and-take that was lively, unrehearsed, and natural. There was no question about it: They were quite effectively sparking off each other.

And that led Arsenio into a discussion of something he had always wanted to talk to her about. He said. It was her image, as portrayed by a photograph in *Vanity Fair*. In the picture one of Madonna's breasts had escaped the confines of her dress. Was she aware that she shocked people by her public display of her own flesh?

"I guess I like to have fun," Madonna said thoughtfully. "I think most of it is the shock value." Then she giggled. "If you've got it, flaunt it!"

But Madonna would not let the issue rest there. She wanted to point out the absurdity of making a big issue out of a naked female breast—especially in the enlightened year of 1990.

"When a guy knows he has a great upper body," she said, "he takes his shirt off. A respectable girl isn't *supposed* to take her shirt off." Why not? she seemed to be asking.

The question that hung in the air was never answered. Arsenio had someone else he wanted to talk about. But he knew how to get a laugh out of the audience during the transition.

Arsenio: "Yours are real!"

The crowd cheered.

That led Arsenio to a quick cut: "Neither of us believes that La Toya [Jackson]'s breasts are real."

Prolonged discussion about female breasts followed, including talk about La Toya's—she's Michael Jackson's sister, of course. Then the conversation veered back to "Vogue" again, and the album.

Soon Arsenio Hall was asking Madonna about the song "Hanky Panky," whose lyrics concern being spanked for sexual thrills.

"I'm talking about the kind [of spanks] you get when you're not bad," Madonna told Arsenio. "The kind you get when you're good." Describing them, she said that they weren't painful blows at all. "Not so it hurts. Just a little stinging."

Arsenio then turned the talk to the motion picture *Dick Tracy* and the character of Breathless Mahoney as conceived by Madonna. A raw cut from Disney Studios was shown to the appreciative audience, and then Arsenio zeroed in on Warren Beatty.

"On behalf of men everywhere—what's Warren Beatty got that we haven't got?" he asked her.

She squirmed just a bit at that question. Hemming and hawing in a most uncharacteristic fashion, she seemed to be trying to think of some clever riposte. Finally she admitted that it was a tough question to answer. Arsenio kept digging in on her, reminded her that Beatty was probably at home right now, watching her on television and waiting for an answer.

"He's not threatened by me," Madonna said finally, thinking it out slowly. "I'm a very outspoken gal and he's not threatened by that."

That broke the ice. It was an intelligent answer to a difficult question.

The banter began to flow in a more orderly fashion. "Joan Collins said [Warren Beatty] was sexually insatiable," Arsenio pointed out.

"He was twenty years old at the time," Madonna said, referring to the Beatty-Collins affair. "Aren't all men insatiable at twenty?"

Is Warren Beatty "satiable" now? Arsenio wondered.

"I would say he's satiable," Madonna admitted.

And you?

"Yes."

He came right after her. "Does Joan Collins make you jealous?"

"No. Have you seen her lately?" Madonna snapped back, quick as a wink.

The crowd went mad over that remark—admittedly a coup de grace—giving it the loudest cheer of the entire evening.

Now it was Madonna's turn to go after her host.

"How does it feel to be dumped for John Stamos?" she asked Arsenio. Arsenio had been dating Paula Abdul, but she had appeared with a performer named John Stamos at the recent Grammy Awards.

Arsenio had no answer. Madonna continued to pile it on until finally he moaned to the audience: "Oooooh! You're telling all my business!" He meant *private* business.

The two continued in lively fashion, Madonna teasing him and Arsenio wriggling helplessly like a fish on a hook. The teasing involved fan magazine stories, including some playful debunking of a tabloid tale concerning an alleged homosexual affair between Arsenio and his friend Eddie Murphy.

"Hey!" Arsenio injected. "There was a rumor about you, too, but I didn't ask you!" Arsenio was referring to a hint on a recent David Letterman show that Sandra Bernhard and Madonna were sexually interested in one another, and a later continuation of the rumor caused by a gag dance the two did together at a public benefit in Brooklyn.

At one point host and guest even discussed several surgical stitches that Arsenio had on his left hand. "What's that from?" Madonna asked brassily. "Too much spanky?"

Laughter.

Things began winding down, but Madonna was not through yet. At one point she gazed at Arsenio thoughtfully, noting particularly his hairdo with its straight sidewalls and flat top.

"If any of my dancers got their hair cut like that," she said slowly, "they couldn't be in the show."

Arsenio's eyes widened. He was taken aback, rendered speechless. But then he went after her. Why not?

"It's tired," she said.

The host fumed and fussed. "What should I have?" Arsenio snapped. "Hair like Warren Beatty's? Talk about tired!"

As the session ended, Madonna had her exit line ready. She cast a glance at the furniture on the set, and then turned to Arsenio, telling him it was old-fashioned and tasteless.

Stunned, Arsenio let her roll on. Then, finally, he tried to call a halt to it, asking her why she didn't like the couches.

They were, Madonna told him, couches you might see in a furniture store window with a sign on them: "Marked half off."

The crowd broke up.

When the show finally came to an end, Arsenio Hall,

the proud host, showed his teeth to the crowd. "You sure got your money's worth tonight."

"There's no denying," Bob Remington wrote, "that the sometimes raunchy three-bleep interview was one of the most enjoyable pieces of talk-show television to drift into living rooms in some time."

Then: "It was all rubbish, but the studio audience went ga-ga." And so, apparently, did the viewers in their own homes.

Even with all the ribbing he got, Arsenio thought the show a great success. "Arsenio loved it," Marla Kell Brown, his producer, told the press the next morning. "He told me today, if he could have her back on the show tonight, he would. For Arsenio, it's his perfect kind of show—unpredictable and spontaneous."

Brown confessed that no one had really known how the interview would go.

"Sometimes when you book a big name and you build it up, you worry [if] they'll live up to everyone's expectations. But [Madonna] *surpassed* them."

Asked later why he let Madonna rib him so unmercifully on the show—teasing him about his relationship with Paula Abdul, laughing at his hairstyle, and even hinting that he was gay—Arsenio gave this response:

"If Madonna stops enjoying herself, then I'm an ass," he said. "If Arsenio is the victim, it's good TV."

However, he did admit that it was hard for him not to let go a zinger or two at her.

"I had a devil sitting on one shoulder saying, 'Crush this girl's world,'" he said. "And I could have done it. I've made people cry and run out of a club after heckling me."

Later, he gave *Ebony* magazine a few "choice words for the pop star":

"First, Madonna," he said, "I will never have to work for you because I have as much money as you have.

"Number two, I've seen your dancers and I'm nothing like them. They work *for* you. I work *with* you.

"Point number three is you wanted to be black when you were little but you were not black, so don't try to understand blackness. It is not your place to dictate black hair care or fashion. You have borrowed our sound but not our sensibilities, so don't make an attempt to tell me how I should look."

But that was long after the fact. On the show he kept his mouth shut. And because he did, he remained true to the purpose of his onstage persona.

"What you've got to remember about Madonna," he said, "is that this is just fun and games."

Arsenio was overjoyed when Paramount announced the debut of *The Arsenio Hall Show* in January 1989. Paramount had also recently released the hit movie *Coming to America*, in which Arsenio starred with his close friend Eddie Murphy.
(AP/WIDE WORLD PHOTOS)

Arsenio considers Eddie Murphy "the brother I never had," so he was thrilled to be the one to present Murphy with his People's Choice Award as favorite comedy actor for his role in *Coming to America*.   (AP/WIDE WORLD PHOTOS)

Arsenio never shied away from controversy in his talk show. Here he hosts singer Sinead O'Connor just after she raised a ruckus by refusing to sing the national anthem at a concert. She appeared on the show to explain her plans to boycott the Grammy Awards ceremony, despite the fact that she received four Grammy nominations, because she considers them too commercialized.
(AP/WIDE WORLD PHOTOS)

Arsenio feels that other late-night talk shows neglect African Americans and makes a point of having guests of all colors on his show. Heavyweight champion Mike Tyson, with his promoter Don King, appeared on the show after Tyson defeated British fighter Frank Bruno in a defense of the world title.
(AP/WIDE WORLD PHOTOS)

Roseanne Arnold was a guest on Arsenio's show when the two comedians finally decided to bury the hatchet and put an end to their public feuding. Arsenio had made Roseanne the butt of many jokes about fat people, and she had fought back by calling Hall "trapezoid head," among other epithets.
(AP/WIDE WORLD PHOTOS)

Veteran actor Robert De Niro chose *The Arsenio Hall Show* to make his first TV talk-show appearance. Arsenio managed to score this coup in his very first season on the air.   (AP/WIDE WORLD PHOTOS)

Arsenio clowns around with good friend and fellow talk-show host Joan Rivers. Hall got his first big break on the late-night circuit when he briefly replaced Rivers as the host of *The Late Show*.   (AP/WIDE WORLD PHOTOS)

Arsenio has fun with the cast of *Cheers*, dousing Woody Harrelson during an on-air water fight. He had the cast on the show to celebrate the two hundredth episode of the popular sitcom in November 1990.   (AP/WIDE WORLD PHOTOS)

Arsenio knew he'd finally made good on his dream of being as popular as his idol, Johnny Carson, when he was recognized with a People's Choice Award in 1990. (AP/WIDE WORLD PHOTOS)

Hall proved he was not only a premiere talk-show host but also a first-class actor with his performance in *Coming to America,* which earned him an Image Award from the NAACP, presented by Clint Eastwood. (AP/WIDE WORLD PHOTOS)

Arsenio welcomes his close friend Earvin "Magic" Johnson to *The Arsenio Hall Show*. Johnson appeared on the show for his first public discussion of his family's reaction to his AIDS test. (AP/WIDE WORLD PHOTOS)

"I was born to do this," says Hall. "When I'm in the spotlight, I'm gone. I love it more than anything in the world. . . . It's the best feeling I've ever felt." (AP/WIDE WORLD PHOTOS)

10

Having a Ball

Even though the usual nightly guest list of *The Arsenio Hall Show* became a rather interesting combination of street-smart rap artists, country singers, geriatric or about-to-be-geriatric movie stars, sports personalities, and sexpots seemingly selected with one eye on the headlines of the supermarket tabloids, the overall mix was actually geared to mainstream appeal, but with an eclectic collage to attract almost every demographic group.

One night the show pitted talk-show host Sally Jessy Raphaël against jazz singer Bobby McFerrin, percussionists Sheila Escovedo and her father, Pete Escovedo, comic Rick Ducommun, and Morey Amsterdam and Rose Marie from the old *Dick Van Dyke Show*. Talk about hedging the bets!

The most consistent programming was drawn from a large group of minority artists who were represented either sporadically or not at all on the other talk shows. In addition, Arsenio's programmers loved to launch young comics who had never before had a chance to wow a mass audience.

Pretty soon it got to be chic for stars like Anita Baker,

Tony Danza, and Farrah Fawcett to telephone Arsenio Hall ahead of time, asking to be put on the show. But the real breakthrough came when even the supermarket tabloids began picking him up for headline news:

ARSENIO PURSUES ROBIN GIVENS
ROARS MIKE [TYSON]: "I'LL KILL HIM!"

And so on.

When Arsenio Hall appeared in a cameo role that was not much more than a walk-on in Eddie Murphy's film *Harlem Nights,* Murphy's directorial debut, Arsenio had Murphy on the show to plug the film and its cast of Redd Foxx and Richard Pryor.

The picture was not faring well at all. *USA Today* warned the unwary: "Don't go if you're offended by gutter language—this one is so thick with obscenities that it was tough to find clean clips for ads."

Jeannie Williams, the paper's critic, was kinder to Arsenio than to Murphy. "Arsenio Hall gets the yuks in a cameo as a mobster who can't stop bawling because he thinks Murphy has bumped off his brother."

Arsenio's showcasing of Murphy helped Arsenio as much, possibly more, than it helped Murphy and his ailing film. Eddie Murphy *was* the big draw on those first shows. Arsenio kept reminding the audience tirelessly that Murphy was the "number-one box office draw in the world."

"Having Eddie Murphy as a best friend is hard," he admitted.

Asked how he handled criticism that he continually name-dropped Eddie Murphy into every conversation possible, Arsenio responded, "Have you ever mentioned your brother's name in conversation? *He's* my brother. The closest man in the world, probably, to me."

When asked to name another close friend who could give some real insight about him, Arsenio avoided the question. "You don't know how much I would like to give you a name, somebody who is close. But I don't trust people. When I first met Eddie, that was the thing about us—nobody was using anybody. I've seen Eddie lose friends because people are hanging around him because they want something. It's a real problem, what people want."

Whenever their schedules would allow, the two of them would dine together or take in an act at a comedy club. But they would never go bowling together. Murphy was a bowling fan of the highest order; Arsenio hated the game.

"He calls me all the time," Arsenio said, asking him to go bowling with him. "Yo, man," Arsenio always answered, "bowling's bull. When you're ready to not bowl, we can hook up!"

In spite of Arsenio's reluctance to name another close friend, he certainly did have one. It was Magic Johnson, the superstar basketball player then with the Los Angeles Lakers. "Magic is the closest thing I have to a man friend," he said, in clarification, pointing out that he still considered Eddie Murphy a *brother,* rather than a *friend.*

Arsenio was introduced to Magic Johnson soon after his arrival on the West Coast by a mutual acquaintance, who started the whole thing by saying: "You want to go to a basketball game? Magic Johnson's a friend of mine."

Of course Arsenio agreed, and when the game ended the friend took him downstairs to the locker room to meet Johnson.

The basketball great stared at Arsenio a moment, and then his face lit up. "Yo!" he said, recognizing him. "The guy from the Comedy Store!"

The identification was acknowledged and the Laker star grinned. "Where did you sit tonight?"

Arsenio cocked an eyebrow. "You see this blood dripping out of my nose? I was *real* high up. Some stewardess from American Airlines came by with peanuts and shit!"

And the two of them continued to kid each other, establishing a friendship that solidified into a permanent relationship.

"Magic says, if you ever want tickets, call him," Arsenio's friend advised the next day, and Arsenio took Johnson up on it. And vice versa. Magic Johnson would come to the Comedy Store; Arsenio would watch the Lakers on Johnson's freebies.

Arsenio confided in Mark Harris, an *Entertainment Weekly* writer, that the two of them were very good friends.

"He's a really special, unselfish kind of guy," Arsenio said. "I don't use the word 'friend' loosely, because I think people use it too much. If I have enough friends to count on one hand, I'm a very lucky man. Magic's one."

Another of the big stars who got on immediately with Arsenio was Whoopi Goldberg. In their conversation, Arsenio proved that he could indeed draw out a star from behind her protective covering.

ARSENIO: How is your life? . . . What do you look for in a man?

WHOOPI GOLDBERG: Truth.

ARSENIO: How do you keep your man monogamous?

GOLDBERG: I just trust he's going to do the right thing.

ARSENIO: Plan on getting married anytime soon?

GOLDBERG: No. . . . I just got divorced. It's taken three years to get it cleaned away. It was tough to get him off. It's like getting gum off your shoe. Then they want something. They come in with air, and they're going to leave with a house and a car.

ARSENIO: Hey, I'll visit you at your house on the ocean. I'll pop down [there] and we'll [lie] on the beach and scare your neighbors.

She appeared time and again on the show, and her skill at repartee proved every bit as natural as Arsenio's.

When the two began having it on with each other verbally, they seemed to forget there was an audience.

On the strength of Whoopi's natural charisma, she was approached by Paramount to hostess her own talk show. The original idea was for her to follow Arsenio Hall, acting as a kind of Letterman to Arsenio's Carson.

At a National Association of Television Program Executives convention at which syndicated shows were peddled to local stations, Arsenio heard one of the executives say:

"Arsenio's become a little *too* black, and Whoopi is the answer to that."

When Arsenio related the story to Whoopi, the two had a good laugh over it. Unfortunately, the plan for the Paramount show never got off the ground, and after some discussion the idea of linking Arsenio and Whoopi soon collapsed.

However, plans progressed for Whoopi to star in her own talk show at a later date.

In spite of the star status of the guests, the audience itself became more and more a part of the general festivities on Stage 29. Revving up the people sitting in the bleachers became a part of the Arsenio Hall tradition; from the moment he appeared, he was all over the stage, cranking his fist above his head, pointing to certain people in the audience, and making a lot of racket to get everyone pumped up to the proper party level.

One night a woman in the seats threw a pair of red lace panties onto the stage. Arsenio went over and picked them up, folded them meticulously in a square, and tucked this into his outer breast pocket. He carried the scarlet emblem with him for the rest of the evening.

By now Arsenio had found that he could work the audience in much the same manner as his father had worked his congregation, creating a magnetic field of excitement between performer and viewer, effectively gluing the observer to the set.

Although Arsenio never roams the audience the way Phil Donahue does, or Oprah Winfrey, he occasionally sallies forth into the bleachers to engage in conversation. Performing sight unseen with people whose viewpoints and attitudes are unknown occasionally presents him with a problem.

"One night I came up to a woman who was sitting next to a guy much younger than her." That was an opening for Arsenio—and he took it. He was thinking of a reverse May-December match-up.

"Who's the gentleman with you?" he asked the woman. "One of Cher's ex-boyfriends?"

The woman looked at Arsenio calmly. "I don't know him. My husband died a month ago."

The audience held its breath. The silence stretched tight.

Arsenio swallowed hard. "I said to myself, 'Agh, Agh.' And it was, Boom, okay, Arsenio, just deal with it. Improv! Do what comes natural."

"I'm sorry to hear that," Arsenio said very quietly. "I'm glad you came today."

The woman smiled. "I watch you every night. When my husband was alive, he used to watch you. You made him laugh."

What could have been a disastrous situation turned out to be a touching moment. Arsenio said, "You take those risks, and people love it."

As the show progressed through its first year there were complaints from some viewers and critics. The show had a built-in black sensibility to it, but some viewers thought that, in its day-to-day execution, it seemed to be featuring *too* much black.

Certainly Arsenio was more likely to kid about James Brown or Whitney Houston than about Dan Quayle or George Bush. Some said that watching Arsenio's show was like hanging out at a party to which one wasn't invited—at which one didn't even know the *language*.

That criticism annoyed Arsenio. Did that mean that it was all right for Johnny Carson to feature white sensibility consistently, and force blacks, Hispanics, and other minorities to adjust to that, but not for Arsenio Hall to feature black sensibility on his show and let the whites adjust to that?

"That mentality," Arsenio said, "keeps television from expanding to higher levels, and expanding to other people." White people who felt that way, he said, obviously couldn't imagine "what it's been like for us for all these years."

He suggested that his critics "sit down for a minute and try to understand my show as a huge amount of what white America is doing, like I did when I watched my first Bob Hope special, my first *Three Stooges* [show]. My whole culturization requires that I understand everything that America is.

"My show is not a black show, it's not a show to take over the airwaves, it's a show to say, 'Let's share the medium now.' . . . Beaver's dead, baby. Beaver's gone. And it's time to let some blacks move into that neighborhood."

Two months after the show's premiere, Arsenio booked Joe Clark, the controversial New Jersey high school principal on whom the motion picture *Lean On Me* was based.

The interview did not have the usual backings and fillings that most such encounters involved; instead it was a straight take-out in which Clark was allowed to give his own side of the argument that ensued over his behavior after the picture was released.

Michael Renov, an assistant professor at USC's School of Cinema-Television and an expert on avant-garde television and film, thought the appearance was a significant departure from the usual late-night fare.

"Joe Clark," he reported, "was allowed to be the person he is, the hyperbolist, the dramatist." Renov believed that in spite of the seriousness of Clark's mission in life—educating black youth—his manner and attitude could have made him a laughingstock on a show hosted by a less sensitive man than Arsenio Hall. Arsenio accepted Clark on his own terms and let him speak his piece the way he wanted to.

Not all the good selections came off as well, however. At first, Arsenio had a hard time persuading some entertainers even to come on his show at all. He had lined up Gregory Hines, the actor-dancer, to promote his motion picture *Tap,* but something happened on the way to Stage 29.

After Arsenio had signed him up, David Letterman's staff got in touch with Hines and convinced him that he should appear on *Late Night with David Letterman* before he appeared on Arsenio Hall's show. That left Arsenio to find a last-minute replacement in a matter of hours. The sitcom *227* was being taped in a nearby studio on the Paramount lot. Arsenio's people swooped down and grabbed up the actress Jackee [Harry] as a substitute.

Everything worked out all right—but Arsenio was miffed.

There were also memorable bloopers on the show. When Michael Douglas and Danny DeVito appeared to plug their movie *The War of the Roses,* Arsenio managed to put a big hole in their proud ship of state. The pair had gone through dozens of interviews without revealing the surprise ending of the picture. Although DeVito had asked Arsenio not to divulge the ending as a matter of course, Arsenio forgot and mentioned it on the December 14, 1989, show.

DeVito bounced up in shock. "You just lost us millions of dollars!" he howled.

Arsenio apologized abjectly after the show and offered to bleep the comment out of the master tape. However, it was not done. When the supermarket tabloids learned what had happened they gleefully came out with stories that De-Vito and Douglas had flipped out because of Arsenio's slip and had threatened to boycott the show forever.

By that time Arsenio was worried that the two actors were mad at him; they were worried they had offended their host. Finally DeVito's publicist, Stan Rosenfield, made an official announcement. "Nobody's mad at any-body." DeVito was just "joking" about the millions of dollars. Some joke!

Then Arsenio's publicist said: "It's a huge statement that these two legends would care about the feelings of a young talk-show host."

The appearance of Dan Rather on *The Arsenio Hall Show* was, according to one critic, "truly bizarre." Diane Holloway of the *Austin American-Statesman* wrote that Rather strode out on Stage 29 to a huge ovation, took off his jacket, and greeted his host expansively. Grinning at the camera "like a Cheshire cat," he proceeded to answer all of Arsenio's questions with exaggerated sincerity and a grin flashing off and on "like a light bulb."

Holloway said that Rather's obvious discomfort reminded her of Richard Nixon on television—the forced smile, the shifting eyes, the grim attempt to appear calm and relaxed. "Who would have thought that Rather, renowned for his tough reporting on the Nixon White House and the subsequent Watergate scandal, would one day be described as Nixonian?"

Arsenio treated the CBS anchor reverently. Rather treated the questions with kid gloves on, underlining his firm belief in civil rights, pointing up his admiration for Martin Luther King, Jr., and Nelson Mandela, and even came out for rap music.

Listening to rap, Rather said, could help people from totally different cultures to understand one another better. However, he added that he was *not* keen on the "vulgarity" of some of the lyrics.

Most weird was a discussion about the blurred line between news and entertainment, with Rather stating his firm belief that the CBS news should be straightforward news, and that entertainment had no place there.

Holloway felt that it was somewhat bizarre to view a nationally known news anchor discussing straight news on an entertainment talk show—the usual purlieu of movie stars, musicians, and other Hollywood-type celebrities. "The whole visit seemed inappropriate."

But Rather's visit got the ratings up.

Hall even managed to orchestrate a little controversy on his own show. Kim Swann and he decided to book Andrew Dice Clay, a comic known for his irreverent racial humor, his antifeminist jokes, his homophobic comments, and, most of all, his vocabulary of four-letter words.

When Clay had appeared on *Saturday Night Live,* Nora Dunn and Sinead O'Connor boycotted the performance and refused to appear. Now he had just made a feature film, *The Adventures of Ford Fairlane,* and was anxious to promote it. And so arrangements were made for his appearance on *The Arsenio Hall Show.*

Starr Parodi, the second keyboard in Michael Wolff's group, refused officially to play the night Clay was scheduled to appear.

"As an employee of *The Arsenio Hall Show,*" she said, "I cannot show my disapproval of Clay by turning the channel, but I can refuse to play in the band, which is a function I have performed for every guest that has appeared to date."

Parodi's advance decision to boycott the show made the papers, and the media advanced on Arsenio's show to watch. Why would Arsenio Hall, who is black, put on an allegedly racist comedian? journalists wondered.

Dana Freedman, the show's publicist, answered for Arsenio. "It is Arsenio's opinion that banning a comedian from his show . . . is not the way to handle the situation.

Rather, his preference is to deal with the comedian's attitude head-on."

As the show started, Parodi was present, playing in the band, but when Arsenio announced Clay's appearance, she walked off the set.

Arsenio said: "I respect her decision."

Clay came on and everyone waited for the bleeps to begin. Clay fooled them all. He quieted down the rather boisterous studio audience and began talking about himself.

"Who's Dice? Who is Andrew Clay? Who's the Jewish kid?" he intoned, getting dramatic and almost self-pitying. "Andrew Clay is a guy who came out here about ten years ago and broke his ass, you know what I mean, *broke his ass,* believed in himself, and became the hottest comic in the world."

After this tearful start, Arsenio and his guest worked the dialogue for everything it was worth. About Parodi's walkout, Clay shrugged his shoulders. "People do what they have to do," he said.

Then Arsenio got in a few licks.

"I've seen your act," he told Clay. "I watched and got a little uncomfortable. . . . Do you have second thoughts about racist humor? What if you were in a club and a guy told an anti-Semitic joke?"

"It's been done," Clay answered, brushing the smoke out of his eyes as his cigarette smoldered in the corner of his mouth. "It's a joke. . . . I love this country. We give everybody an opportunity. In Manhattan, every fruit stand is owned by a Korean, every cab is driven by a guy in a turban and a jewel in his head."

Clay sighed. "I don't talk about anything that doesn't exist."

Arsenio asked Clay a pointed question: "Where do you think you'll be in twenty years?"

Clay answered: "I'll probably be the biggest box-office draw ever."

When it was all over and the critics went after Arsenio Hall the next day, he shrugged them all off.

"The bottom line [in this business] is, if I kept everyone off the show who said something racist, I'd be doing monthly specials."

Since that time, Arsenio's lenient attitude toward Andrew Dice Clay has hardened. It was, he told *Entertainment Weekly,* a "mistake" to have him on the show. "Racism by any name is still racism."

He admitted that he had watched the man do jokes on the handicapped that he would never do, but, since Clay was not "messing with black people," Arsenio thought it was all right for Clay to joke about "Asian people and gay people and people with AIDS."

Then one day, he said, he saw a tape of a Clay concert. Some of Clay's AIDS jokes were so reprehensible that Arsenio concluded: "I've been wrong and irresponsible."

So, no more Andrew Dice Clay appearances for *The Arsenio Hall Show.* Arsenio's self-confessed schizophrenia seemed to be evidencing itself. Or perhaps he was simply proving to himself that he could—like anybody else—simply change his mind if he felt like it.

Arsenio himself looks back on his own actions on the show sometimes with a jaundiced eye, revealing that schizoid persona. Sally Kirkland was on his show one night, gushing over him.

"I think you're wonderful!" she told him.

"I can tell," Arsenio responded, eyes and teeth agleam. "Your nipples are hard."

Embarrassed silence. Then big guffaws.

Arsenio notes that he went too far that time. Never again.

Most celebrity "feuds" are phonies. For years Jack Benny and Fred Allen carried on a fabricated and carefully crafted feud on radio. Conflict hypes ratings. Arsenio did have a few feuds on his own. But only one of them, according to a recent statement, was genuine.

"The only person I legitimately ever feuded with was Roseanne. That was real."

Roseanne Barr—later Roseanne Arnold after she married her second husband—is a television sitcom favorite. The feud with Arsenio apparently started after Roseanne had appeared on the show a couple of times. The two entertainers got along fine at first. Then Tom Arnold somehow got into the act.

By this time Arsenio was using Roseanne's name to punch up a number of fat jokes. Barr, hearing about it—or perhaps tuning in on the monologues and hearing them herself—became incensed.

And so, backed by her husband, Roseanne decided that she had as much right to insult Arsenio as Arsenio had to insult her. At first her jokes were kept within a small circle of intimates. However, things did not remain that way for long. She went public during a People's Choice Awards Ceremony in 1990, making several pointed jokes about Arsenio's sex life. The quips were excised from the final broadcast of the show.

As Arsenio told it, "She did a joke where she said there have been great comedy teams in the world: Lucy and Ricky, George and Gracie, and Arsenio and Jim Nabors. Now that is a very hip Hollywood joke to say that I'm gay and I'm sleeping with Jim Nabors. When you challenge a black man's manhood there are no rules anymore."

The feud then broadened when Arsenio began to show photographs of Roseanne Barr on his show. Taken by a freelance photographer, the pictures were of Roseanne Barr in a swimming pool with her husband, Tom Arnold.

Then, in May 1990, the photographer sued Arsenio for violating his copyright on honeymoon photographs he had taken for the Arnolds, even though they had appeared in the *National Enquirer.*

Soon after that Roseanne Barr claimed that Arsenio Hall was a racist. She insisted that when he poked fun at people who were fat, he was indulging in a form of racism.

The feud simmered through the summer. Finally, Arsenio himself told the press that maybe he had gone too far in making jokes about Roseanne's weight.

"I felt that maybe I was a jerk. So I stopped."

However, he did not apologize for being a racist.

"Fat people weren't brought from fatland and forced to work free and separated from their fat relatives and hung from large trees. I don't buy *that*."

Finally, in October 1990, Barr and Arsenio sat down to talk and make up. By that time Barr had described Arsenio as a "triangle-headed [obscenity]."

The talks, at which Tom Arnold was present, were hardly of the summit variety. But they did settle the dust.

"We went and saw him," Arnold reported. "And we all had a long talk. Rosie felt really good about it. . . . It's not like we're talking about Iraq or anything. This is just two comedians who were feuding."

11

Hip and Flip Beat Chic and Sleek

"**O**ne bad show, and I'm mentally packing a U-Haul," Arsenio Hall once said. "But I don't want to start playing it safe. I accept the fact that I can't have it forever."

And yet . . .

"I was watching *The Tonight Show*. Somebody was hosting for Johnny. Jimmie Walker was the guest." When Arsenio was in high school, J.J. Walker was the hottest thing going. But now, on *The Tonight Show,* he was nothing more than a middle-aged man looking back and saying, "I could have been."

"I remember crying," Arsenio says.

Then there was a cable special in which people walked by the same Jimmie Walker and joked: "That's Arsenio Hall." Because Hall was *hot* and Walker was *not.*

Arsenio: "It's scary. Someday I'll be the punch line."

Hey, speaking of punch lines, what ever happened to *The Pat Sajak Show*?

The race between Arsenio Hall and Pat Sajak developed in January 1989 just about as expected. Sajak came out way ahead of Arsenio simply because of the enormous amount of publicity that CBS-TV had arranged to promote the show. After all, it was a matter of prestige for that network to come up with something that would be real competition for Carson.

And the strategy worked exactly as predicted . . . for a while.

Jeff Jarvis of *People* magazine reviewed the two new shows in the January 30, 1989, issue.

"Pat puts on a show that is at least aggressively okay, sometimes downright good. And he's getting better by the day." He gave the show a grade of B +.

"The [Hall] show is too hyper, too huggy, and none too bright. The problem: Arsenio is trying too hard." He gave him a C +.

At the close of his review he went so far as to predict that Arsenio Hall might not even survive his own show.

Jarvis felt that while Pat Sajak was "nice to have around," Arsenio Hall was far too obsequious to the celebrities he interviewed.

The *People* assessment, while not exactly accurate on a long-range basis, was fairly on target for the initial performances of the competing hosts. For the week of January 9, 1989, the first week in which the two new show hosts were slotted head-to-head with Carson and Letterman (in New York), the figures looked like this:

Carson and Sajak were tied, both NBC-TV and CBS-TV scoring a Nielsen TV Index of 5.3. Letterman (who followed Carson and was not directly in the competition) and Hall were tied for third place with 3.1. In several of the earlier nights, Sajak actually beat out the mighty Carson, but these were sporadic victories. And the equivalency figure in the ratings proved soon to be a chimera, simply an afterimage of the huge mass of publicity that had been generated to launch the show.

Bob Wisehart of the Newhouse News Service assessed

the Sajak show somewhat differently from Jarvis:

"I was there for the January 9, 1989, maiden voyage of *The Pat Sajak Show*—one of several hundred jammed in banked rows that stretched almost to the ceiling of the refurbished $5 million Studio 42 at the fortress-like CBS complex called Television City."

However, as Wisehart watched Sajak walk through the curtains to ecstatic applause that gathered momentum and shook the rafters before subsiding, he noted that the host seemed "awfully small, a little frail, and a touch tentative."

The way things turned out, his impression of a shrinking Sajak was on the button. Even on that initial night, the Carson show was not too concerned about the new kid on the block. Johnny Carson took the night off. Jay Leno, then his permanent guest host, subbed. Those first nights Arsenio Hall was not even in the running.

Sajak's gangbusters start annoyed Arsenio Hall over at Paramount, down the street from CBS's headquarters. He knew Sajak's lead had been engineered by hype. "Why were they pulling so hard for Pat Sajak to succeed [against Carson], instead of me?" he asked. "Why? Is it because I'm black?"

The luster quickly faded from Sajak's show. By the end of January 1989, there was visible evidence backstage at CBS-TV that the executives and stars of the show were beginning to plunge into that vortex of desperation that could precede a slide into oblivion if countermeasures against such a calamity came up short.

It was obvious that Pat Sajak's amiability at the *Wheel of Fortune* was not of the translatable variety; while he might be able to spin a roulette wheel with a fair amount of finesse, it was not necessarily true that he could spin a web of interest sufficient to ensnare and captivate a sleepy talk-show audience.

One critic put it this way: "Sajak, as amiable a character as any to show up on television, is, frankly, a bore. His humor skirts between artificial and innocuous, a combination of nickel-and-dime routines and bits that would be tossed into the garbage can in the offices of David Letterman's writers."

Also, he was not a solid interviewer in the manner of the great talk-show hosts. He seemed at the mercy of his guests, quavering like a bird dog to move on to the next commercial so as not to screw up the evening's revenue schedule.

The *Chicago Tribune* said: "Visiting his show—and watching late-night chat fests is very much like dropping in to a party—is like going to a bash thrown by friends of your parents."

And yet all the top executives at CBS-TV were confident of ultimate success. They had to be; they were committed. "The Sajak show is a top priority with us," Jeff Sagansky, CBS's entertainment president, told a press conference.

Howard Stringer, Sagansky's immediate superior, echoed the positive thinking: "We have a strong commitment to the show."

In spite of all the brave words, the aroma of flop sweat permeated the atmosphere. Stringer brought in Kevin Stein and Michael Wiseman to help out. Stein was named director of CBS Late-Night Programs. Wiseman, a former NBC sports president, would be coexecutive producer of the Sajak show.

At the same time, Sajak's writers began composing self-denigrating jokes about an "ax hanging over [Sajak's] head"—enough to prompt Arsenio Hall, on his show, to make a promise not to tell any more Sajak jokes—"[because] I feel bad for anybody's failure."

When the Sajak show premiered, of course, everyone at CBS-TV had hoped that Pat Sajak just might have the talent to lure viewers away from Johnny Carson. But no one expected that an unheard-of comic from Cleveland might appear to change the whole look of late-night chatter. Plus which, no one expected a *syndicated* show—broadcast to a large degree on independent stations and at various times in the night—to beat out a *network* gem.

A review early on by Merrill Panitt in *TV Guide* outlined the direction of the battle between the two concepts. First Panitt stressed the similarities between the combatants:

Both hosts featured hip show-biz talk, a plethora of anecdotes, inside gossip on celebrities, and mutual appreciation. Each was charming, witty, and charismatic. Both men seemed to be up to the tasks they had undertaken for themselves.

Then he got down to the individuals.

Pat Sajak, he said, was droll and charming in a cute, personable way. He obviously knew where the camera—and the viewing audience—was, since he played to it shamelessly. He was self-deprecating, unpretentious, and because of those attributes, generally appealing.

When Charlie Sheen talked about his own "serious involvement" with the police, Sajak rejoined: "I certainly wouldn't want to break a time-honored talk-show tradition and ask a follow-up question, so we'll just let that go. No problem at all." And that, the critic pointed out, left viewers all over America hanging by their thumbs.

Sajak's producers at CBS had him doing walks, interviews, and gimmicks outside the studio, à la David Letterman. One night he even took a stroll through the farmers market adjacent to the studios, where he made sharp, well-crafted wisecracks to visitors eating or shopping there. Forays like this usually worked well, Panitt wrote.

Arsenio Hall was more of a stand-up comic whose stock in trade was making faces and doing odd bits of mimicry to hype up his anecdotes, which, in Panitt's view, were mediocre at best. He criticized Hall's tendency to overpraise his guests, naming especially comics and Brat Pack film stars. There was also a pandering to the studio audience, whomping up whoops and screams with the mention of certain favorites. He called the studio audience "the most annoyingly loud" in the history of talk shows.

In conclusion, Panitt asked rhetorically: "Are Hall and Sajak as entertaining as Carson? Not yet."

Even by the end of January 1989 it was obvious that Sajak had lured a few people from Carson's compound, but Arsenio Hall had attracted a whole new untapped generation of viewers to the late-night talk battlefields.

To add insult to injury and cast *People* magazine's prophecy into the clouded crystal ball category, Arsenio Hall was in the process of turning the ratings race into a personal triumph. His face soon appeared on the cover of *Time* magazine, *Rolling Stone,* and the *Boston Globe* and *New York Times* magazines. Even *People* magazine!

Sajak was being ribbed for his recent marriage at the age of forty-three to a former *Playboy* model named Lesly Brown, nineteen years younger than Sajak.

The contrast between the two hosts could not have been more pointed. Their close associates—the support group—though never seen by the viewing public, clearly reflected the images of the hosts. And it was Sajak who came up short in the comparisons.

His warm-up comic, John Melchor, appeared nightly in a starched, button-down shirt, typical of the uptight executives who made up the yuppie Sajak staff. Arsenio Hall's warm-up comic, Daily Pike, came out in a stylish Hollywood zoot suit, modified from an earlier West Coast era, but zippy and chic—just right for Arsenio's image.

At an interview, CBS's Stringer observed that Arsenio Hall had "demonstrated that the way to success in late-night is to counterprogram. We're going to try with a livelier, more mobile show [for Sajak]."

Promises notwithstanding, that livelier, more mobile show did not surface in the following months. By April the reek of failure was heavy in the air at CBS headquarters. The changes came quickly and dramatically in an attempt to plug up the holes in the defenses. In the case of the Sajak debacle, there were too many leaks to be plugged.

The first to suffer the heat of cauterization was Dan Miller, Sajak's designated sidekick. His presence became a black hole. He vanished from sight, becoming no more than a disembodied chuckle that seemed to emanate from some dingy cell in an adjoining dungeon.

The ambitious ninety-minute format was next to go. It was slashed to an hour—paralleling the fate of the original Johnny Carson show.

The set also underwent cosmetic surgery. The old desk-and-couch seating arrangement was replaced by a table and chairs, an obvious concession to Arsenio Hall's overstuffed couch and chair setup. But the table and chairs failed to resemble even an old lady's tea setting; in effect, it resembled nothing at all. Wags called it a "Sajak sitdown."

In April, Sajak's ratings had dropped to 2.9. Hall's had risen to 3.9. In July, Carson was still in the lead with 5.4. But now *Hall* was second, with 4.3, Letterman third with 3.1, and Sajak last with 2.8.

During the summer Hall even led Carson in the three top big-city markets.

By January 1990, CBS-TV knew it had a major problem. The brass decided it would have to eat the $5-million refurbished studio it had created for Sajak, plus the $6 million it had dealt the star.

In April 1990 Sajak went on vacation to Europe, where he was when the announcement was made at CBS-TV. No one in the know was particularly surprised at the news. *The Pat Sajak Show* was canceled as of Friday, April 13. One newspaper led off the story with this paragraph:

"It's funny how the man who would be Carson isn't even Sajak anymore. And it's even funnier that Johnny Carson didn't do Pat Sajak in; Arsenio Hall did."

Pat Sajak's dream of returning to the good old days of Jack Paar, Carson's predecessor on the show, when the "sheer power of good conversation" was enough to nail couch potatoes to their sets for an hour, was a good one—but it didn't work in the world of 1990.

Shortly after the demise of *The Pat Sajak Show, US* magazine ran a survey to find America's favorite late-night TV talk-show host. To the surprise of some, but not everyone, Arsenio Hall was chosen by the magazine's fans. Hall won out in a poll of 3,600 readers.

Taking advantage of the empty slot in the late-night talk show arena caused by the departure of Pat Sajak, ABC-TV immediately hired a Los Angeles disk jockey named Rick Dees to appear in a show called *Into the Night with Rick Dees.*

The Rick Dees show was scheduled to follow Ted Koppel's *Nightline,* the half-hour interview show that ended at midnight.

Meanwhile, CBS-TV was not standing short. Originally, the network announced that it would showcase a number of new talk-show hosts in late-night slots during the coming summer, including two Chicago radio stars named Steve Dahl and Garry Meier, and a comic named Joy Behar. The series would be called *The Midnight Hour.*

For the fall, the network planned to feature five action-adventure shows—one for each weeknight.

ABC was not at all happy with Hall's rising popularity. Its St. Louis outlet made plans to drop *Nightline* and replace it with *Arsenio* because ABC would not allow the Koppel show to be pushed back ninety minutes to make room for it.

The television pundits tried to determine where Arsenio Hall was really heading. The Nielsens showed that he had built up an audience between the ages of twelve and thirty-four to the point where Sajak's show collapsed. That audience was, to advertisers, an important one, since it comprised a ratings group that bought high-volume items like records, cosmetics, soft drinks, and blue jeans. About half of the audience was female, a favorite target of advertisers.

That put Hall in contention with Carson, because Carson's audience—though larger than Hall's—was skewed to *older men,* not exactly the greatest of all purchasing groups. Also, Arsenio's popularity was high in urban centers, while Carson's was not necessarily so.

An executive from the McCann-Erickson advertising agency, Joel M. Segal, discussed Arsenio Hall's skin color, which, he said, did *not* come into play at all. "He's a crossover personality, a mellow kind of personality, not just black."

The two shows were no match yet, however. *The Arsenio Hall Show* was appearing on far fewer stations than *The Tonight Show.* Hall had 175 to Carson's 208. Because of the fact that it was syndicated, *The Arsenio Hall Show* appeared at different times throughout the country—from 11:00 P.M. to 1:00 A.M.—a variable that affected the potential size of the audience.

Plus which, Arsenio Hall had never said he wanted to bury Carson. The worst thing he could do, he once said, would be to topple the master.

"I don't want to have America turn on me because I'm in the way of something that is a tradition. I'm just willing, like a kid, to wait my turn. The mistake that Alan Thicke and Joan Rivers and Pat Sajak made was to design a situation just like Johnny's—get a desk, a guy beside you. You can't out-Johnny Johnny. You can't knock off a legend. Why try to take Johnny's audience? I just want their kids."

And now he had them.

12

The Liar and the Pimp

"**Y**ou can kill your strongest enemy with love," Arsenio Hall's grandmother used to say to him, paraphrasing Martin Luther King, Jr. And Arsenio often said that that was the way he tried to fight those who did not like him.

"The more someone comes at me," he told Patrick Goldstein in *Rolling Stone,* "the more I give them my smile."

However, Arsenio did not always turn the other cheek. One of his early targets proved to be that most celebrated of all black filmmakers, Spike Lee, who was on the show to promote his highly touted film *Do the Right Thing.* The confrontation between Lee and Hall was, in fairness to Lee, not all his doing.

It was Arsenio who leaped right in at the beginning of the exchange, cross-examining Lee on a number of negative positions he had taken, especially his critical appraisal of other black entertainers.

One of Lee's targets was Whoopi Goldberg. He had scored her for wearing blue contact lenses to make her eyes

146

less dark. He suggested that it might be because she was kowtowing to whites, making herself more like them to win their approval. To him, that meant she was demeaning herself and being patronizing to her white audience.

As soon as Spike Lee was settled into the overstuffed couch, Arsenio began the conversation with an in-your-face question: "What's your problem with Whoopi Goldberg?"

Lee finessed the question by avoiding any direct engagement with his host. But Arsenio wasn't through quite yet.

"What's the beef between you and Mr. Murphy?" he went on.

Spike Lee had criticized Eddie Murphy for not translating his enormous box-office clout at Paramount Pictures into something tangible for other black entertainers—like forcing Paramount to hire more blacks for jobs on the lot.

Arsenio had aired Lee's reproaches on his show with Murphy as a guest one night. Murphy, remaining well within the parameters of the sharp-tongued cop character he had created on the screen, responded to the charge by remarking that Spike Lee had all the "sex appeal of a cricket."

After saying that it was unfortunate that Murphy was not present to speak for himself, Arsenio said that as Murphy's best friend, *he* would speak *for* him.

"Even someone with Eddie's box-office power can't change Hollywood overnight," he told Lee. "And that change doesn't occur any quicker if you go to a Caucasian journalist looking to stir up conflict by telling him what you think of your black brother."

He referred to the fact that Lee's comments about Murphy had been put in print by a white reporter.

On the show, Spike Lee kept his cool and departed without firing a shot. However, it was obvious that he was simmering below the surface. About a week later, when he

was back home in New York, he told reporters at the New
Music Seminar that he thought Arsenio Hall was nothing
more than a modern-day Uncle Tom. "He's obsessed with
hugging white women," Lee said. His remarks were later
broadcast on MTV.

Lee had been scheduled to appear for a second time
on *The Arsenio Hall Show,* during which Hall planned to
question him in more depth and let him speak his piece.
However, listening to a replay of the MTV broadcast,
Arsenio instructed his people to cancel Lee's scheduled appearance.

"I gave him my platform the first time to publicize his
film, and my initial thought after hearing what he said on
MTV was, 'I wish I could grab this little maggot and choke
him.' The biggest tragedy is that it's black people fighting."

On a radio program Arsenio then admitted that he was
annoyed when Lee hung the Uncle Tom label on him, even
though it was well known that Arsenio Hall hugged almost
everyone on his show, from Ringo Starr to Sly Stallone,
and from Whoopi Goldberg to Danny Glover and dozens
of others.

"Maybe a ghetto ass-whipping will teach him not to
talk that stuff!" Arsenio snapped.

Several days after that, the two contenders found
themselves sitting near each other at a charity all-star basketball game sponsored by Magic Johnson—one of Arsenio's very special friends. That was where the Hall-Lee
hatchet was eventually buried.

The two shook hands. Spike Lee said: "We're never
going to be best friends. All I have to say is, 'God bless
him and I wish him all the luck in the world.'"

Arsenio Hall did invite Lee onto his show again, and
all went well between them. About the filmmaker, Hall
later said: "I know what Spike's game is. He's got this
blacker-than-thou thing going. He's the new Malcolm and
everyone else is a money-grubbing hustler. It's B.S., that's

what it is. Spike would love to have my audience. He'd
love to have Eddie's audience. What would you rather
have? *Beverly Hills Cop* or *School Daze*? Me and Eddie
have become targets for people like Spike."

Arsenio Hall had a lot more to say about black-bait-
ing. "There just aren't enough successful black people [in
the business] that we should be attacking each other to
white journalists. After two hundred years of slavery, there
just isn't enough time to worry about Whoopi's contacts. I
felt the only way to drive this point home was for me, 'Mr.
Happy,' to call him on it. But it wasn't a message just for
Spike. It was for all of America. Imagine how powerful this
country would be if we weren't fighting with each other all
the time."

In *Playboy* magazine, Arsenio assessed the Spike
Lee–Eddie Murphy bout in more detail. "[Spike Lee] accused Eddie. He said any man who makes a billion dollars
should demand more black participation at Paramount."

And he continued, "Standing on the outside doing
She's Gotta Have It, you don't understand the big leagues.
If Eddie went in and told [Paramount chairman] Frank
Mancuso to do something, he'd tell Eddie to fuck off."

Arsenio elaborated with a smile: "I've *seen* Eddie go
in and demand things, and they've said, 'Fuck off.'

"It takes time to get things." He was serious again.
"And you can't demand them: You have to slowly show
the need, show them it makes money. 'Cause the bottom
line is, there's not as much racism in this town over 'You're
white and I'm black' as there is over 'Show me green.'
Trust me: The biggest racists in this town will give you anything you want if you show them a profit."

In all, Arsenio Hall regretted his actions toward Spike
Lee, admitting they showed signs of his own immaturity.

"I responded like a kid from the ghetto in Cleveland,
instead of like the executive producer of *The Arsenio Hall
Show,*" he sighed. "It was very important for me to shake

Spike's hand at the all-star game and let him know I wasn't like that." In retrospect, he commented that mouthing off at Spike Lee was "the wrong way [for me] to handle it."

Spike Lee was not the only black person with whom Arsenio Hall found it difficult to get along. Even before his show was launched by Paramount he found himself enmeshed in a controversy with Willis Edwards, then head of the Beverly Hills/Hollywood chapter of the NAACP. Edwards was engaged at that time in a struggle with the national headquarters over an investigation into possible mismanagement violations in his operation of the chapter.

Edwards's first move in the confrontation with Hall was a published statement that he was "outraged" that the new *Arsenio Hall Show* had no blacks in "key behind-camera positions."

Arsenio did not respond until a week later, when he pointed out publicly that the reason he hired people was because of their qualifications; no qualified blacks had applied for the jobs he had filled with whites. It was that simple, he said.

Edwards quickly offered to help Arsenio find qualified blacks. No action was taken on either side, but the simmering feud did not cool down of its own accord. In an interview in the Los Angeles *Sentinel,* a black newspaper, Arsenio claimed that Willis Edwards had started this confrontation by (allegedly) trying to "extort" a $40,000 donation to the NAACP from him.

Now Edwards held another press conference and claimed that Arsenio Hall had been "on a campaign to dog my name," and in turn filed a $10-million defamation suit against Hall. The defamation occurred, Edwards said, when Hall wrongly accused him of being an "extortionist."

Arsenio then denied that he had used that term. He said that Edwards reportedly asked him to donate money to avoid a bad report from the NAACP about not hiring more blacks on his show.

Jose De Sosa, the president of the California state chapter of the NAACP, then demanded an apology from Arsenio Hall for slanderous remarks about the organization and about Willis Edwards.

"The bottom line," Arsenio then said, "is that I have more blacks behind the camera and in front of the camera than anyone else in the history of talk shows." He also pointed out that he had enough trouble overcoming the obstacles whites had placed in his path without having to overcome those placed there by blacks in their attacks on him.

To *Rolling Stone,* Arsenio Hall personified Willis Edwards as a "phony motherfucker black-tennis-shoe pimp."

Eventually Edwards resigned from the presidency of the Beverly Hills/Hollywood chapter of the NAACP and filed a *second* $10-million defamation suit, including *Rolling Stone* in this one for publishing Hall's description of him.

The first of the defamation suits was dismissed in March 1990 by Judge Ernest Williams of the Los Angeles Superior Court. In the decision, the judge said that Arsenio Hall's comments about Edwards, which appeared in the *Sentinel,* personifying Edwards as an "extortionist," were protected by his right of free speech.

But the judge also said that in the confrontation between the two men, both had engaged in "name calling," and that any claims of defamation would have to be examined in that context.

"For example," the decision read, "evidence shows that [Edwards] called [Hall] a 'bold-face liar.' Evidence also shows that [Hall] reportedly called [Edwards] a 'black-tennis-shoe pimp.' Calling [Edwards] an extortionist fits within this name-calling context."

Nevertheless, in spite of the heavy press coverage and the unusual hassle between these two men, Arsenio Hall survived the bad press and even managed to come out on top in the public's view. By resigning from the hot seat of the troubled Beverly Hills/Hollywood chapter of the NAACP, Edwards seemed to bear the brunt of any public opprobrium generated by the feud.

But within Hall's psyche there was always an ambivalence about political considerations. And even though his father had been a minister, Arsenio often exhibited a wariness about supporting Jesse Jackson, who was also a minister.

"He's a great orator," Arsenio said of Jackson. "But I don't know if he has the political skills from his background that it takes to be president [of the United States]."

Other than that, Arsenio Hall was generally noncommittal about politics.

Sexual politics were a different matter. And Arsenio Hall did not always come out on the right side, particularly when it came to *black* sexual politics.

"I did his show once," said the actress Anne-Marie Johnson, "and I'll never do it again because it's a very nasty atmosphere." Johnson plays the role of Althea Tibbs on TV's *Heat of the Night*.

"[Appearing on the show] was terrible," she said. "You know how he abuses people—women specifically. And women who don't act like bimbos who want to sit on his lap, and, you know, take their bra off. It was very insulting."

She said she was told by the producer to sit on the couch with Arsenio and just be herself. "Great," Johnson thought. "It'll be wonderful and warm."

But on the set, when she came out, he shook her hand and said: "God, you are so skinny!" It was the *way* he said it that bothered her. But that was not all. The first thing he brought up was the fact that she was now dating a white man; what, he asked her, had happened to her black boyfriend?

She was unnerved by the question and could find no adequate way of dealing with it. "He has a problem with [black] women dating white guys," she said. "So I'm tap-dancing, trying to get out of that, and [Arsenio Hall] looks over to the imaginary stage manager, and looks [back] at me."

According to the actress, Arsenio told her, "Well, your time's up. Thank you very much. And I don't like the way the light's looking on you, so why don't you stand backstage?"

She simply walked off, promising herself never to appear on the show again.

No one on the show would comment on Anne-Marie Johnson's remarks. They appeared in the *Ottawa Citizen* under the byline of Jay Boyar of the *Orlando Sentinel.*

While Arsenio Hall may not be eloquent about sexual politics, especially black sexual politics, he could always be eloquent when questioned about black pride.

"There's a subconscious racism that's been driven on blacks so hard that it's become part of their attitude about everything," he observed. "But you cannot become part of the oppression. I want to hear black people say, 'I can do anything!' I'm not one of those guys who uses the word *nigger* for fun. And I don't use it onstage to entertain. Never."

He went on. "I am angry. I'm on a tightrope, and people are punching me from every direction. I give 110 percent. I resent the fact that for some white critics I have to be whiter to be a star." Pause. "And then there are the jabs from my own people, the implication that I have to be unfair to whites to make blacks happy."

As if that wasn't enough, in November 1989 Arsenio Hall trod on another land mine and found himself in the news once again. His stand-up monologue involved a joke spun off from an incident at Los Angeles International Airport.

Security agents had swooped down on a suitcase that had been red-flagged for possible terrorist activity when it traveled through the X-ray machines at airport security. The suitcase was inspected by security guards who found a Nintendo video game cartridge in it that, on the films taken by the security equipment, resembled a bomb.

Arsenio used the news item in his monologue, suggesting that someone might easily be able to pass through airport security "to meet Allah." In naming that "someone," he used an obviously Muslim name.

Forty Muslim pickets showed up in front of Paramount Pictures the next day, protesting Hall's material. The protesters were incensed that he had used a Muslim name in his monologue because, by doing so, he had allegedly depicted Muslims as "terrorist bombers." The group demanded a public apology.

However, Arsenio did much on his own to combat racism. When the three major networks in 1990 more or less ignored the celebration of the life and works of slain civil-rights leader Martin Luther King, Jr., *The Arsenio Hall Show* made a special effort to pay tribute to King.

His staff booked a white gospel singer, Amy Grant, to pay a musical tribute to King and paired her off with 1960s folk singer Dion, then backed the two of them up by selecting more traditional choirs and nontraditional rap singers to round off the program. Dion—born Dion Di Mucci—was to perform his 1960s hit, "Abraham, Martin, and John," a tribute to King, Abraham Lincoln, and John F. Kennedy.

"It's going to be a musical tribute to Martin Luther King," Arsenio told the press. Yet he did not want to make it seem as if the tribute was especially targeted at a black audience. That was the reason he had selected Amy Grant and Dion over many other black performers.

"Martin Luther King is an idol of mine," he said, "for a lot of reasons. I don't want to go into it, but everybody has their idol, and he's mine. Anyway, I wanted to do a couple of interesting things.

"First of all, when I talked to [the show's talent scout] I said, 'We've got to do a tribute to Martin. The Bible says, "Make it joyful."' I think it can be a great gospel/musical tribute. But what's most important, appear to make the tribute represent *all* of America."

He went on, "Martin Luther King is a black man who's a hero to me, but I also think what he did was important to all of us. That's why I sought out Amy Grant and Dion."

Arsenio was once quoted in *Playboy* magazine as saying, "I was told by black people, 'Hey, I watch you and I love you, man, but lemme tell you, white man ain't gonna give it up to you.' But America—*white* America—is watching me. It's like a scary dream, that people are choosing this black kid from Cleveland over the legendary host of *Wheel of Fortune.*"

13

The Hollywood Closet

Each comic performer usually works out his own routines and character roles, patterning the material on a few primary favorites. Johnny Carson was Arsenio Hall's role model, no question about that. But Arsenio had other comic favorites as well.

One of these was Flip Wilson.

Arsenio favored Geraldine over Flip Wilson's gallery of other characters. Wilson, he thought, had down all the nuances of speech, gesture, and facial expression as he played Geraldine in drag. What Arsenio borrowed from Geraldine was Wilson's use of the falsetto voice. He did not create a separate character as Wilson had done, but instead lapsed occasionally into the falsetto black female voice when his stand-up material called for it.

It was Arsenio's shtick to interrupt his narratives as he told an anecdote and to dramatize the dialogue by lapsing into different voices. The Geraldine voice was his favorite for any woman he might be playing. He simply extended his voice range up about two octaves and minced the words.

156

Arsenio Hall created another voice for his male characters, since he wanted to make his people identifiable over and above the tone he used to tell the story. Thus if he quoted a man, he would lower his voice about two octaves and roll out a kind of macho tough-guy version of the American male of the streets.

With these two basic "other voices," Arsenio could generally bring off his routines without further delving into the complex art of voice impersonation.

Occasionally, however, he found it expedient—and laugh-provoking—to mix the mincing Geraldine voice with the male voice in order to personify the homosexual male. Because most comics can extort a laugh by playing a mincing homosexual, Arsenio was guilty frequently of lapsing into the affectation in order to pump up a laugh when the material might prove too flimsy to carry the routine.

He was certainly not the only comic who occasionally got himself out of the doldrums by slipping into the affectation of the flaming homosexual, but he was one of the first to be publicly confronted by gay activists and accused of being a homophobe, a hater of homosexuals. One routine in particular may have provoked this.

This routine, which was aired in December 1990, concerned a lesbian- and gay-pride parade that was held in Los Angeles. He described it for what it was, and said that its purpose was to celebrate "whatever the hell it is they celebrate."

He then proceded to make stereotypical gestures to indicate homosexuals and commented that the heterosexuals watching the parade through West Hollywood acted like American tourists on safari in the lion country of Africa, in that they frantically rolled up their windows to protect themselves.

The response came on Friday night, December 14. Arsenio had gone through his monologue, had fired up the audience in his usual manner, and was returning from the

second commercial to interview Paul Hogan, the Australian
actor who had made the character of Crocodile Dundee an
international favorite, when a group of gay activists in the
audience made an unscheduled appearance.

It began when someone from the audience threw out
a line for the host. Hall did not hear the exact words and
frowned out into the dark.

"Huh? I'm sorry. I didn't hear you, man."

The camera caught sight of a man standing in the audience wearing a T-shirt with the words "Queer Nation" em-
blazoned across his chest.

The man shouted out clearly: "Why don't you ever
have any gay guests on your show?"

Arsenio stared right back at the heckler. "Why don't
I have any gay guests on my show?" He thought about it
for a second. "What? I'm sorry. Why don't I have any gay
guests on my show?" he repeated in order to set up his
answer.

There was silence from the heckler.

"Well," Arsenio went on, "there are a lot of gay
guests who really don't *like* to talk about their sexual preference, so we don't know whether they're gay or not."

This answer seemed good enough for the audience,
which applauded him.

With that, it seemed that the show would continue.
After a few seconds, however, it became evident that Arsenio was annoyed. He did not want this interruption and
his response to go without a clincher. He had been on the
defensive. He decided to counterattack.

"Now," Arsenio said with a soft smile, "this ain't
Merv. You didn't think I'd run from this, did you? This
ain't Johnny. I ain't going to run from it. I'm going to deal
with it."

The audience clapped briefly, although actually, they
seemed to want the show to continue with the featured
guests, but Arsenio was getting wound up. "I don't know

Gus Van Sant, but I know Elton John," he said. "He's been here and he's rocked the house." That seemed to put paid to the heckler's argument that there were no homosexuals on the guest list. "Okay?" Arsenio asked, staring at the heckler.

More applause. Let the show go on.

Arsenio Hall was now in command and he was about to march. "This is my show, okay?" he told the heckler. "This is *my* show!"

And let's get on with it, the audience seemed to say.

"You think I haven't had somebody on the show because they're gay?" Arsenio said to the heckler. "What's wrong with you, man? I'm black! I'm black, man! I'm black, man!" In each instance, he put a different emphasis on the word. "I'm the biggest minority you know about!"

But Arsenio was just getting up steam.

"I don't want to hear that gay trash, man! I've got gay friends I've had on the show. Because you don't know them or they ain't who you want on the show, you got a problem with it? If you want to book it, get yourself a show!"

That seemed crushing enough, and Arsenio was ready to get on with the interview with Hogan. But he realized he had been saying too much. After all, people were tuned in to him for entertainment—not a lecture. And the audience seemed a bit uneasy around him.

"I apologize to you sitting out there," he said into the camera, referring to those tuned in, "and you sitting here. It's rude and it's out of order. The one thing I would not do is discriminate against a guest because of his sexual preference."

Arsenio paused as if he were going to return to his material. Then he turned again, staring out at the group in the audience that had begun the diversion. "But it ain't none of your damned business that they're gay!" he shouted.

The audience applauded.

But Arsenio, who was now warmed up, was far from through. "Why is it," he asked rhetorically, "that you can do a joke about anything and anybody, but when you do a gay joke, I've got to have idiots in here protesting over it? You don't see Dan Quayle here."

Applause.

"You don't see Milli Vanilli here. What's your problem?"

More applause.

"I apologize for myself," he said again, "and I apologize for them. Let's move on."

But even when Paul Hogan showed up and began talking, it was not over.

Arsenio Hall was still simmering. "I'm a *brother,* man," he broke into the conversation suddenly. "Nobody knows more about discrimination than I do. Believe me, I have gay guests. I have gay employees. I don't give a damn [about sexual preference]. I just want to entertain."

And that was the material that appeared on the taped syndication that night. Getting to the bottom of the problem was no easy matter. The staged demonstration against Arsenio Hall apparently resulted from an invitation sent out by his production company to attend a new show of which he would be overall producer but would not appear in it. What irritated the gay rights activists—members of Queer Nation—was the statement on the invitation that said attendees would come as guy-girl couples. That, to Queer Nation, appeared to be an indication that Hall was not truly sympathetic to homosexuals.

But there was also the material Arsenio had used in his stand-up routine about the lesbian- and gay-pride parade. After that aired, the Gay and Lesbian Alliance Against Defamation (GLAAD), a media watchdog group, had written to Arsenio Hall and his producers for nearly a year, they said, without any response. Attempts to communicate with him were unsuccessful.

"They've never responded at all," said Richard Jennings, executive director of GLAAD's Los Angeles chapter. It was for these two reasons that Queer Nation mounted the attack on the show.

In order to quell any rumors about his homophobia, Arsenio then had several avowed homosexuals appear on the show, one of whom was the actor-playwright Harvey Fierstein. Fierstein came dressed in a flowing caftan.

About the caftan, Fierstein told Arsenio: "I'll let you try it on later." After some amusing patter, Fierstein, speaking in his distinctive gravelly voice, gave the Queer Nation's thematic moral:

"Gay people should be allowed to be as dumb and boring as you heterosexuals." Then, after a pause, to Arsenio: "You should hear me in the morning." Another pause. "Maybe you will."

But even though the situation was defused, it did not go away. Arsenio scheduled Andrew Dice Clay for a return engagement on the show on May 16, 1991. This was prior to the time Arsenio finally decided he had had it with Clay's putdown humor. As noted earlier, Clay is an entertainer with a shtick of antifeminist, antiminority, and anti-gay material. He has even sometimes espoused violence against women and gays.

The night of the Andrew Dice Clay show Paramount's security reported to Arsenio Hall that someone had recognized a known member of Queer Nation in the prospective audience. Security suggested barring his entrance along with a number of people with him, all wearing Queer Nation T-shirts concealed beneath their outer clothing.

Arsenio was annoyed, and at first agreed to block out the group. But he then decided that he might well have a repeat of the December 14 incident, so he opted to let the potential protesters in and to try to defuse the situation before the taping began.

Arsenio later defended his decision. "I thought that

[keeping them out] might not be the right thing to do. I thought the better thing might be to let them in and make an attempt to communicate."

Just before the show started, Arsenio appeared before the studio audience and announced that there were a number of people, including members of both Queer Nation and AIDS Coalition to Unleash Power (ACT UP) who were opposed to Clay's presence on the show, since Clay was a controversial figure in the entertainment business.

"I need you to trust me to hold the thing together," Arsenio told the audience, "and represent everyone's question and point of view."

He went on to say that the problem in Hollywood was not heterosexuals like him, but closeted gays.

Even so, there was one particularly vocal Queer Nation member who would not keep silent. One of Clay's handlers requested that Arsenio's producer remove that offender from the studio. It was Arsenio himself who nixed that idea. Clay finally acquiesced to the person's presence in the audience.

In the long run, Arsenio explained, he was in the entertainment business. "I think my responsibility is to give the person to the public, ask the questions, and let the public decide. It's an exchange, but it's not by any means a vote."

When the show began taping, he tossed out his prepared monologue and did a Phil Donahue–style audience exchange, giving Queer Nation members, ACT UP members, and fans of Andrew Dice Clay a chance to speak.

Afterward, his interview with Clay turned into a serious session and included questions about Clay's brand of humor and whether it encouraged violence against women and gays.

According to Bruce Mirken of *The Advocate,* a magazine oriented to gay readers, "Hall's strategy worked: The issues got aired, and, except for a handful of shouts from the audience, the taping went without interruption."

Arsenio Hall confessed to Mirken later during an interview that he was a "slave to ratings" and to Hollywood establishment standards.

"I can satisfy every group and get canceled and not satisfy anybody. You know the phrase 'between a rock and a hard place'? Well, I'm caught in a motherfucking avalanche. I had a woman tell me the other day I don't have enough pretty black women on the show. You have no idea how I break my ass to give people what they want."

Arsenio told Mirken that many gay entertainers asked him not to discuss homosexuality. "You'd be surprised how many people come to the show and say, 'I don't know if Arsenio is aware of . . . but would you please not get into it?' Please don't fault me because the people who come on my show don't choose to talk about their sexual preferences."

Arsenio Hall admitted that he sometimes slipped up. "When I've had people say, 'I didn't like that gay joke,' my response is, 'I've made mistakes.' And when I do, I try not to do it again. I've soul-searched. Every joke that I do angers someone, so I search my heart, and unfortunately I have no apologies to offer right now."

Nevertheless, he pointed out, "I don't do Dice Clay–type jokes about gay people. I believe if my gay friends come on the show, I don't have to take them out." (He meant take them out of the closet, reveal their homosexuality.) "I hear gay jokes that, as a heterosexual man, bother me. I've heard jokes that could make a man go out and punch somebody in the face, and that bothers me. I don't think I'm a bad guy—if I were, my gay friends would tell me."

No matter how equably he tried to handle the homophobia accusation, he felt he had been unjustly singled out for attack.

"The thing that amazes me is that Johnny Carson just

did thirty years [as talk-show host]. Have I done less than him in bringing these people to the air? I've never seen Queer Nation jump up at Johnny Carson. Sometimes I watch my show and say, 'Johnny never had to do this.'"

Queer Nation's attack on him, Arsenio felt, was a "racist assault." "They'd never do that to a white man. They've never done it to Johnny; they've never done it to David Letterman. I probably have the largest gay and female staff in this town, and you've got an organization coming to me and saying I'm prejudiced. Bullshit! I have respect for the struggle of the Queer Nation, but please don't end my career with your struggle."

But there were among the gay activists still those who thought there were problems. Queer Nation took exception to Arsenio Hall's notion that the group was engaging in a "racist assault" on him. Its membership was by no means all white, in spite of the fact that no blacks took part in the demonstration.

Also, these advocates pointed out that the group had good reason to single out Arsenio Hall for confrontation rather than Carson or Letterman. "Arsenio Hall does fag impressions," Yoav Shernock, a member, commented. "No one else does that on national TV."

Another protester assailed Hall for blaming everything on the studio heads. "[Arsenio] has some control, and he can have the balls to take a stand," said Wrene Robyn. She pointed out that Hall's show was one of Paramount's biggest television successes, bringing in over $70 million a year in advertising.

GLAAD's Jennings was disturbed by the fact that the show's audience is composed mostly of eighteen- to thirty-four-year-olds—and that because of that, Arsenio Hall was "making hate hip" for the youth of America.

Overall, however, it was decided that the protest came out a plus for everyone concerned. Mark Kostopoulos, of ACT UP, said: "I thought it went very well in that real issues were discussed. Issues of how humor affects homo-phobia, sexism, and racism were discussed on national tele-vision."

Arsenio noted that there are limitations to the discus-sion of complex social issues on a talk show, which is pri-marily entertainment. Nor is it a suitable medium for the exploration of national and international issues.

"Ted Koppel is a journalist," Arsenio Hall pointed out. "I'm just a guy from Cleveland. I ask real ordinary Midwestern questions."

In no way, said Arsenio Hall, was he antigay.

"People who have problems with me don't know me."

But they were getting to know him better.

Cory Roberts, who organized the action for Queer Na-tion, noted: "Opening up the show the way [Arsenio Hall] did was a very positive step. That doesn't mean we won't be watching him."

This last comment, published in *The Advocate*'s July 1991 issue, initiated a loud rejoinder from Arsenio Hall.

"Watch my black ass!" he told *Entertainment Weekly*. "I have hard-working friends who are activists for gay rights who believe that that approach is detrimental to the gay community, because what America sees on the news is violence and anger. There is a way to do it without ostraciz-ing people who could be warriors on your side."

As for being a homophobe: "That's ridiculous. If I were homophobic, I'd lose half of my staff and a lot of my guests. It's as simple as that."

14

A Black Fairy Tale

One day during President Jimmy Carter's administration the shah of Iran made a visit to the White House, trying to drum up support for his shaky regime in the Middle East.

Columnist Art Buchwald, walking past the White House, was somewhat surprised to note that presidential security had allowed a number of demonstrators onto the White House lawn while the visiting potentate was being entertained in the Rose Garden. The activists were parading about with brown paper bags over their heads—making identification by police difficult—screaming through mouth holes for the deposition of the shah.

Buchwald's imagination began to soar. He thought of what might happen if indeed the shah *were* deposed while he was away from Iran. He could never go home again, could he? Naturally, that would not bother the shah of Iran; he had money to burn. However, what if he were a potentate of an oil-rich nation who was worth only what he had access to while he was shah? What would happen if he were set adrift in the United States without a penny to his name?

166

Toying with this basic idea and elaborating on it freely, Buchwald in March 1982 completed an eight-page treatment for a motion picture about an African ruler of an oil-rich country who is deposed while visiting the United States. As a spoiled-rotten rich despot, what would happen to a man made suddenly penniless—especially if he became entangled in the coils of a woman agent of the CIA?

He showed his treatment to a number of film people, among them the French director Louis Malle. Malle was interested in making the film, but did not have the financial backing. He advised Buchwald to cut the treatment by at least half. Buchwald created a three-page version by the end of summer, 1982, which he then peddled around Hollywood through the usual channels.

In 1983, Paramount Pictures optioned the idea and handed it to producer Alain Bernheim to develop into a comedy for Paramount's up-and-coming black star, Eddie Murphy. The story did not go well, and three scripts—and a half a million dollars—later, Paramount reluctantly dropped its option with Buchwald and Bernheim in 1985.

No particular reason was given for dropping it; the script simply did not fly, and the treatment of *King for a Day,* as the film was tentatively titled, was relegated to the bottom drawer of Buchwald's file cabinet.

Meanwhile, executives at Paramount Pictures were still trying to find a suitable follow-up for Murphy's escalating star status as evidenced by the film hits *48 Hours, Trading Places,* and *Beverly Hills Cop.* They eventually settled on a story about an African prince who comes to America to seek a bride.

The picture—whose working title was *The Quest*—was eventually released in 1988 as *Coming to America,* starring Murphy and costarring Arsenio Hall.

In 1989—one year later—Art Buchwald decided that he had been had, particularly since *Coming to America* had become *the* hit of the previous summer, grossing at least $120 million in its initial release. Buchwald felt the final picture was a direct revamping, without permission, of his original treatment for *King for a Day*. Buchwald sued Paramount Pictures for $5 million for the theft of his story idea; technically he was suing Paramount for breach of contract. Writers David Sheffield and Barry W. Blaustein were credited with the script "based on a story by Eddie Murphy."

In this case, it was thought inappropriate to have Eddie Murphy testify on his own behalf. Instead, Paramount's executives would testify for the studio, and Arsenio Hall would appear as a character witness for Eddie Murphy and also testify to the fact that he had worked with Murphy to devise some of the incidents and characters in the film.

The trial took place in December 1989, less than a year after Arsenio Hall had become virtually a household name as the talk-show host with the fastest-growing popularity on late-night television. Word leaked out that he was to appear at Superior Court in Los Angeles on Tuesday, December 19, 1989, and the media went wild. So did the public.

When Tuesday dawned, the courthouse was under siege. Two special guards were posted, and even before the session began some of the sheriff's female deputies were photographing one another with Arsenio Hall. Other women asked the talk-show host for his autograph and then rushed about the courthouse in ecstasy, waving signed slips of paper in the air. The women were not alone. Male fans went just as ga-ga.

Arsenio commented to the press that the courthouse and courtroom "looked just like television."

Once on the stand, he testified that it was he and comedian Eddie Murphy, not columnist Art Buchwald, who had conceived the idea for *Coming to America* in 1987, four years after Buchwald's original story idea was optioned by Paramount Pictures, and two years after the option was dropped.

Arsenio portrayed Murphy as a "generous, sensitive, and talented person." He said that Murphy had approached him in 1987 to play the role of his sidekick in a film.

In the film, Murphy was to appear "very gracious, very strong, very intelligent. We were going for all the wonderful qualities that a woman dreams of in a man and that a man wants to be," Arsenio said. The idea was to "portray this *positive* image of royalty in Africa."

In discussions with Murphy, Arsenio Hall said, "I basically was listening. We were having a discussion about the fact that Africans in general [have been] betrayed by this town." By "this town," he meant Hollywood.

"As a kid growing up in Cleveland," Arsenio observed, "I never knew that there were skyscrapers in Africa and there was wealth. . . . This may sound funny, but I only knew about the guys who helped Tarzan. I never knew about the riches and the wealth and the dignity."

While Buchwald's story characterized the king as a "spoiled rotten despot," Arsenio pointed out that Murphy's conception was more *likable*. Murphy's idea, he explained, was to create "a fairy tale about love."

In addition, he noted that the leading lady in Murphy's film was quite unlike the CIA call girl in Buchwald's treatment. According to Arsenio, Murphy did not put the most beautiful actress he could find in the role, but settled on a more positive characterization.

"We wanted a certain type of internal quality, mental quality," Arsenio said.

According to his testimony, the story that he and Murphy developed reflected Eddie Murphy's wish to be judged on his acting merits rather than on his fame or wealth.

"You experience a thing in this town of wanting to put that away and hide that so people will deal with you for the person that you are," Arsenio said.

"It was to be a black fairy tale. There had never been

a black fairy tale. We wanted to create like—a fairy tale, beautiful, like the prince got the girl. We wanted a fairy tale *everyone* could relate to."

Hall testified that he knew absolutely nothing about Art Buchwald's treatment of *King for a Day*. He told how he and Murphy would act out scenes and ideas and recite them into tape recorders as they worked together. Murphy drew on his own experiences in portraying the multiple roles. For example, Arsenio said, Murphy's characterization of an old white man was based on director John Landis's father-in-law. Arsenio's own father, the Reverend Fred Hall, served as a basis for the preacher's role Arsenio played.

Later the two actors sent these tapes to two *Saturday Night Live* writers who had worked with Eddie Murphy in New York, David Sheffield and Barry Blaustein, who molded them into the script of *The Quest*.

At one point Buchwald's attorney suggested that Eddie Murphy, who got story credit for *Coming to America*, might have an "ego problem." Arsenio Hall then recounted how one of Murphy's recent films, *I'm Gonna Git You, Sucka,* was developed from an Eddie Murphy idea; for that motion picture Murphy did not seek *any* credit.

"Nobody will ever know that it came from Eddie's idea," Arsenio testified. "He's a very generous man."

Asked why the two stars had worked out the action themselves rather than leave it to the professional scriptwriters, Arsenio said that if the two of them had left the script to others, "it would be just another black story written by white people."

In fact, the key element of the film—Eddie Murphy's change-of-pace role as a reasonable, rather sentimental person—came about deliberately. Such a fairy tale as he envisioned, Arsenio explained, would have no integrity if Murphy were to play his usual con-man character.

"We did a face-lift on his character," Arsenio explained. "He was not the wise-cracking Alex Foley character from *Beverly Hills Cop*. This [picture] showed him soft, sensitive, nonmaterialistic. He was a gentleman. In this movie, he was the perfect man. Any woman would love him."

At one point when Arsenio said that he and Murphy were as "close as real brothers," Paramount's attorney Robert Draper asked him pointedly: "Would you lie for Eddie Murphy in court?"

Arsenio Hall shook his head. "No," he said firmly.

At another point, Buchwald's attorney, Zazi Pope, tried to get the talk-show host to admit that Paramount Pictures was desperate for an Eddie Murphy vehicle to follow up the earlier hits—and would go to any lengths to get a good story.

Pope read from a deposition Arsenio Hall had written out before his court appearance in which he claimed: "If Eddie Murphy wanted to break wind, they would have accepted it as a film."

On the witness stand, Arsenio shook his head. He said the words did not convey the truth. "The 'break wind' [thing] is a joke," he explained. "It's just a joke, kind of a compliment to his talent."

In order to cast Arsenio Hall's testimony in a questionable light, implying that his close relationship with Murphy and Paramount would prejudice him overwhelmingly in favor of Murphy, Buchwald's attorneys pointed out that it was Murphy who, by giving Hall a role in *Coming to America*, had given him his big break in show business.

Arsenio demurred. "What put me on the map was Joan Rivers losing her job." When she failed, he took her place and made his own debut.

Once Arsenio was off the stand, Frank Mancuso, the chairman of Paramount Pictures, took his place in the witness box. He maintained during two hours of questioning that he was only "generally" aware that producer Alain

Bernheim was working on a scenario from Buchwald's treatment. He said he did not remember that it was being worked out for Eddie Murphy, in spite of the interoffice memos filed as exhibits in the case that showed it was so planned.

Asked if the studio was renegotiating Eddie Murphy's contract again, after four increases already, Mancuso nodded. "We are *always* in negotiations with Eddie."

Outside the courtroom, Arsenio Hall told reporters who were crowding around him that he was "offended" and "insulted" by Buchwald's claim of plagiarism.

"I'm offended because Eddie's a very bright man. I am a very bright and talented man, if I have to say it myself. Why do we have to seek a stolen concept? It's insulting. That's what bothers me most."

Many stories had been written about Africa and African kings, he said. "It's very unfair, what's going on [here]. I'd rather loan Art Buchwald some money than go through this."

In the end, Paramount lost the case, but the court absolved Eddie Murphy from blame for the breach of contract.

"*Coming to America* is no less the product of Eddie Murphy's creativity because of the court's decision than it was before this decision was rendered," said Los Angeles Judge Harvey A. Schneider in ruling that Paramount Pictures must pay humorist Art Buchwald for the script idea he claimed was the basis for the hit movie.

"The court concludes that *Coming to America* was based upon a material element of or was inspired by Buchwald's treatment," Schneider wrote in a thirty-four-page statement released in Los Angeles in January 1990.

The judge made it clear that the ruling was not to denigrate Eddie Murphy's creative talents and stressed that Murphy was not wrong in using the term "based upon" in the story credits of the movie. He also said that in no way should Murphy be blamed for the dispute with Buchwald.

"It is Paramount and not Murphy that obligated itself to compensate Buchwald if any material elements of Buchwald's treatment were utilized in or inspired a film produced by Paramount."

The studio made an official statement:

"We don't agree with the judge's decision on the contract claims. However, we are pleased he threw out the claim for punitive damages. We are confident that the appellate court will find that *Coming to America* was created without any contribution by Art Buchwald."

The studio appealed the ruling but lost again, and it was not until March 1992 that the final settlement was made by Judge Schneider. Art Buchwald was given $150,000 for his contribution to the film—a rather low figure in comparison to what he had originally sued for.

Nevertheless, Buchwald's lawyers said that they were not disappointed. "It's close to four times what Paramount wanted to pay," said Zazi Pope. "We won the case. We won the legal ruling. We still consider it a victory."

Alain Bernheim was awarded five times what Buchwald got—$750,000 for his work on the script.

Buchwald reacted positively when asked if he was disappointed at the size of the award. "Sure, if I counted on making millions of dollars, I'd be disappointed," he said. "But I didn't count on that. I'm delighted."

Paramount considered the settlement a victory for them.

"They declare victory every time they lose," Buchwald noted. "They always claim victory. It's cost them between $2 million and $3 million to defend this case."

Legal fees did indeed come to $2,250,000 at final reckoning—a costly victory for whoever really was the winner.

15

The Magic Johnson Show

Earvin "Magic" Johnson, the superstar basketball player for the Los Angeles Lakers, announced on November 7, 1991, that he was retiring from the game. Tests had shown, he said, that he was infected with the HIV virus, which causes AIDS. Although he was in excellent health, he had been advised by his doctors to quit professional sports.

Johnson, long regarded as the most charismatic of the select group of superathletes, a proven champion, and a class-act individual, had been a role model for the young since he had become a star. Facing this shocking truth—that he, like anybody else might have been, was a victim of what some have termed the "twentieth-century plague"—Magic Johnson continued to act like the champion he is.

He made the announcement of his infection and his retirement and took on the awesome responsibility of becoming an ambassador for safe sex through confessing publicly that he had been infected not by high-risk sexual or drug practices, but by the simple act of heterosexual union.

174

He knew that if he did not clarify the truth there would be gossip and speculation about how he had become infected—a fog of misinformation that might doom many others to infection through unsafe sex.

Telling his story took the kind of courage that was the epitome of Magic Johnson's character.

And to help him get his message across to the country—to the world—Magic Johnson immediately contacted his friend Arsenio Hall, on whose program he had appeared a number of times.

Immediately plans were made for him to be on the show the following night. News of his appearance spread almost as rapidly as the news of his retirement. By the time the show aired on Friday night, November 8, millions were watching.

When he first heard the bad news from Johnson, Arsenio burst into tears on the telephone. In handling the interview, the host exhibited good taste, objectivity, and his own brand of personal charisma.

When the show started, the hundreds of basketball fans in the audience greeted Magic Johnson with a two-minute standing ovation. Some of the spectators began a rhythmic chant of "Magic! Magic! Magic!" during the cheering.

Johnson was touched.

"This is the response," he said, pointing out to the crowd. "I couldn't buy what happened."

Arsenio's first question was open-ended, allowing Johnson to tell his story in his own words.

Why, he asked, did Johnson want to come on *The Arsenio Hall Show*?

Johnson: "I want everybody to practice safe sex, and that means using condoms," he told the viewers. "I want everybody to be aware of what's going on."

He went on to point out that a million people have the virus without knowing it. It was one of the reasons he had decided to help educate the public.

"I came on this show to let the people know what time
it is," he said. "Please put your thinking caps on and put
your cap on down there," he continued, gesturing below
his belt.

He told those who were listening that they should not
be afraid because he had become infected with the HIV
virus.

"We don't have to run from it," he said. "We don't
have to be ashamed of it."

As Arsenio looked on, Johnson spoke directly to his
audience of millions.

"You don't have to run from me like, 'Oh-oh, here
comes Magic!' You don't have to feel sorry for me."

Then he told them why.

"If I die tomorrow, I've had the greatest life!"

Arsenio then directed the interview into a much more
delicate area.

"Let's talk about Cookie," he said. Cookie Kelly was
Magic's new wife.

And Johnson did talk about Cookie. He said that
when he told her he was infected with the HIV virus, she
was shocked. He offered to leave her if that was what she
wanted. All she had to do was say the word.

"She almost smacked me upside my head for suggesting it," Johnson said. "She's a strong woman and I was
smart to marry her."

He then explained how his infection had been discovered. He told the audience that he had been taking tests
for a life insurance policy, and the blood samples continued
to come back puzzling. As they were repeated and the sam-
plings became more complex, the physicians discovered the
presence of the HIV virus.

Arsenio Hall switched the conversation just a bit and
began talking about rumor-mongers who might be spreading misinformation about AIDS. He didn't want any of
them to give people the wrong idea about the disease.

"We've all got to have thick skins," Johnson responded. "People can't get me down, nothing they can say. I know who I am. I know what I'm about and they've got to deal with me."

The audience applauded.

"I also have to educate the black community as well, because it's really spreading in the black community," he said.

Then he went on to the important part of his message to the people.

"First of all, I'm far from being a homosexual." His sudden knowledge that he was infected with the HIV virus taught him that there were many myths floating about concerning AIDS.

The most important myth to isolate and stamp out, he said, was the myth that AIDS could happen only to gay people.

"That's so wrong," Johnson said. "I was naive."

He then informed his audience that when he had telephoned Arsenio Hall to tell him that he was going to retire from basketball Arsenio had broken down and wept; in fact, the two of them had cried together.

On the show, Arsenio was embarrassed and agonized at Johnson's revelation of his own emotional reaction to the tragic news of his friend's health.

Johnson then told his host that his mother and father were taking the bad news as well as could be expected. They told him that they still loved him.

This was important for Johnson. He pointed out that he was now living not just for himself and his family, but for a lot of people not even remotely connected to him in a family way.

The segment closed with a tremendous hand for Magic Johnson and for Arsenio Hall as well.

By the time the show was broadcast in all its outlets, Magic Johnson had become the primary spokesperson for safe sex and for waging a battle to control the HIV virus and eventually neutralize the effects of AIDS.

Several nights later, Arsenio Hall strolled through his studio audience and engaged individuals in a discussion of AIDS and safe sex. The audience, composed mostly of young people, both black and white, showed that Magic's revelations had set them all to thinking seriously about the disease.

One young woman said she thought the answer was abstinence. Another said she would try safe sex with condoms. Two black men, who said they were born-again Christians, promised that they would abstain.

Others generally supported the exhortations to use a condom and only clean hypodermic needles. Several pointed out that the danger of contracting AIDS was minimized in monogamous sexual relationships.

Arsenio himself suggested that his teenage viewers abstain from sex until they were older. He admitted that perhaps monogamy was preferable to wide-ranging sexual relationships and said that he himself was supportive of married monogamy—in fact, he was always looking for the right woman to marry.

As for the Magic Johnson show itself, it drew astonishingly high ratings. According to the A. C. Nielsen Company, the segment with Magic rated a total of 9.9 in the twenty-five major markets, the highest in the show's history.

Compared to the Madonna show, which drew a 6.5 overall rating (with approximately six million households tuned in), the Magic Johnson show reached over nine million households.

16

The Power and the Glory

"**I** pray before every show that I can be the best I can be," Arsenio Hall once admitted. "I want to be the Martin Luther King of comedy."

The man who was selected by Magic Johnson to lead him through the dramatic public revelation of his discovery that he was HIV positive was in no way the same man who had some years earlier debuted as a new guest talk-show host on Fox network's *The Late Show,* putting his personality and his career hopes on the line.

That 1987 man was frightened, diffident, worried, and emotionally conflicted, even though it did not show on the outside. He was basically a warm-up comic who employed a special brand of high jinks and comic absurdity that not infrequently crossed the borderline of good taste so he could be *noticed.*

The years between 1987 and 1991 had seen dramatic changes in the persona of Arsenio Hall. His character had matured and his interviewing skills had improved considerably. He had become a man who knew who he was and where he was going—a man who had taken charge of his

179

character formation and molded it into the shape he wanted.

Nor was he diffident anymore about speaking out about himself and about life.

"They say I'm the happiest man in show business, but I'm aware of reality. And the reality is for me to treat people in a way I was *not* treated."

Arsenio Hall then put a positive spin on that with this clarification:

"That's why I put so much emphasis on those people who [were kind to me] without a reason."

He included his show's producer, Marla Kell Brown, whom he had worked with on Fox's *The Late Show;* his talent producer, who had worked with him on Toni Tennille's daytime show; his hair stylist, makeup person, and wardrobe woman, who were people he had met on *Solid Gold;* and, of course, Michael Wolff, whom he had met before coming to Hollywood, and John B. Williams.

Even with Eddie Murphy he had always had a symbiotic and friendly relationship rather than one based on envy and competition. "We found that we could both accomplish a lot more by supporting each other than by trying to knock each other off and deciding who was the best." Arsenio smiled a little and admitted: "We were both achieving success, him at the bank a little more than me, so we understood each other's problems."

Arsenio was always grateful to Joan Rivers, whom he had replaced on *The Late Show* after her exit. Her treatment of him, he noted, was a class act.

"[After Fox signed me on,] Joan sent me letters and cards, telling me I was doing well and advising me about how to handle situations. Quite often, people were told not to do my show because they would disappoint the Lettermans and the Carsons. Joan was the one who told me I was the new kid on the block, so I should take them when I could get them."

And he did, of course.

"You're going to be able to dance and sing with the Temptations," she told him, "you're going to eat milk and cookies with Malcolm-Jamal Warner, and you're going to ask Brooke Shields a question Johnny won't ask."

The result of treating others as he would have them treat him sometimes resulted in criticism. Didn't he put too many of his personal friends on the show?

"I try not to let the critics bother me. . . . When Johnny has Burt Reynolds on the air, there's no problem. When Johnny says, 'We're going to have to play tennis,' there's no problem.

"The problem is, I'm good at what I do and they're trying to punish me." Arsenio leaned back and laughed, unable to resist a punch line. "For the critics' sake, I've been spending more time alone and trying not to make friends."

Of course, sometimes the critics were on the button. "They're right when they say my interviews with Muhammad Ali, Joan Collins, or Sammy Davis seem more like tributes than interviews. They *are* tributes. I'm throwing a party on my show. And when you invite people over for a party, you don't cross-examine them. What do these people want? When I have Stallone on my show, am I supposed to say, 'Yo, Sly, you say you're not a stupid shit, yet you marry this crazy bitch who sends you her picture in the mail, she takes you to the cleaners, and *Martinizes* you!'"

Arsenio shook his head. "I could do that, I suppose, but I won't. I'm Mr. Happy. I'm the Candy Man, doing my best to spread love and laughter. So instead of cracking on my guests, I'll dance to Motown with Maury Povich. If people want the other thing, let them watch *Crossfire.*"

He laughed out loud. "Look. The white press bet big money I wouldn't make it. They said a black show just wouldn't play in white-bread America. They said it so often I started to worry maybe they were right. You know those questionnaires that ask if you're black, white, Asian, or other? I wanted to be one of those 'other' people."

About being "the happiest man in show business," Arsenio admitted: "Although I entertain you every night, I'm also a real person, and life's a bitch! I live to put a smile on your face and make your life a little bit better. This is a very tough world we live in. This is a world where our great leaders like Martin Luther King and John F. Kennedy try to help us, and we kill them. We shoot at our pope and try to kill him and all he says is, 'God bless you.'

"What I do every night is important to bring a smile to your face, because it's a motherfucker of a world we live in. I know some of the people sitting at home laughing have to go out and look for a job the next day. I'll give them this hour, because we *need* laughter. Laughter heals."

Treating others with decency and trying to give them a chance to laugh a little are good missions in life, but Arsenio Hall believed in a great deal more than those two virtues.

"Sure, I'm a bad boy sometimes. But I'm not doing the kinds of things they hear in school. I'm not doing necrophiliac humor. Let's have fun; let's do some humor on the edge. But let's keep our noses clean and keep a positive attitude in our hearts toward a better tomorrow."

He always tried to find a positive line in his comedy. "I've got to be me. If some critics think I'm too easy on my guests, I don't care. I *am* nice. I *like* celebrities. I don't believe half of the stuff you read about them. Like how stupid they are. Hell, you don't get to be rich by being stupid."

Being positive, Hall knew, paid off for him. He had been trained to think positive from birth—not only by his father, but especially by his mother and grandmother. *They* were the ones he always looked back to as important reasons for his success.

"I have a respect and love for women that borders on

an obsession," he said. And that respect and love showed in almost every move he made, particularly on stage.

In a *Village Voice* story Barry Michael Cooper described Arsenio's effect on women:

"It's amazing how the women react to him, both white and Aframerican. Aframerican teeny-boppers screech, and their eyes glaze as they take in his angular, athletic build. Their grandmothers nod their heads with pride at his natty attire: the GQ suits with the slanted cuffs that fall right on the vamp of his nine hundred dollar croc loafers. Makes them think of Duke Ellington and the Renaissance Ballroom again. Young Aframerican women in their twenties, thirties, and forties just straight up and down *lust* after the guy."

Cooper described watching two white women studying him one day, overhearing one whispering ecstatically to the other: "Look at how long his fingers are. And his feet!"

Bonnie Allen of *Essence* magazine wrote: "Everybody wonders whether Hall, who comes across on TV as the most likable guy ever to get near an airwave, is really as nice as he seems. It seems incongruous that he could be loose and open and just-plain-regular. In a business where nice guys don't even get to start—let alone finish—last, humility is not necessarily an asset."

But he certainly had it. Humility and another old-fashioned virtue: love of his mother.

"How could I not be happy [in this career]?" he asked. "I've been able to have my mother come to L.A. and be with me. She's never owned anything, always lived in an apartment. And now she has her own West Hollywood condo. If this guy isn't going to smile, who is?"

Arsenio Hall's love and respect for women went much further than his mother, his grandmother, and his working associates. It went deeply into the heart of his emotional involvement with women in general. But always, his respect for them held him back from being open to the public about his private relationships.

Naturally, the woman question—that is, whom was Arsenio dating, in whom was he *interested*—began looming as a public relations problem once *The Arsenio Hall Show* became popular. The most exciting thing about any entertainer—aside from skills at stagecraft—was always his or her relationship with members of the opposite sex.

From the beginning Arsenio had been rumored to be paired off with almost anyone single in show business—from Brooke Shields to Cher to Whitney Houston to Paula Abdul—but Arsenio never let the rumors become active. Nor did he do anything to stimulate new rumors, as some publicity hacks did as a matter of course to build up new print images for their clients.

"Who I'm sleeping with—who I'm really sleeping with—you will never know," he told *Cosmopolitan* magazine. "In fact, I've never been in love with a performer or had a serious relationship with a performer.

"The stories about Whitney Houston got started because I did jokes about being her 'love machine' in my monologue. One night, I came out and said, 'I'm sorry. It's just a joke.' She came out behind me and said, 'No, it's not a joke. I'm pregnant.' The crowd went nuts, and the rumors started."

Arsenio found it difficult to believe that anyone truly successful could even *have* a family life. He sometimes found himself saying:

"There should be something that looks like you running around the house and a woman who's saying, 'Dear, Irving Azoff's on the phone.' But anyone who's been in a relationship with me in the last five years has complained that I don't pay enough attention to them.

"My fear is that if I had a wife, I'd be a terrible husband to her; I would not give her what she needs and deserves. Because right now, I've got another woman called Show Business, who will leave you if you neglect her. You have to make her number one, or she'll be outta here. I haven't found a woman yet who wants to be the chick on the side."

That was Arsenio's true love—his own show.

"If *A Different World*'s Jasmine Guy"—a good-looking dancer and actress with a piquant face—"yanks me by my one-hundred-percent-cotton collar and growls, 'Marry me,' I'd gasp 'No.'"

Such total dedication to an inanimate love began to worry Hall as his career continued to rise. He admitted that he worried most often about not really being worried about loneliness.

He felt that he should be *concerned* about the fact that most nights after he wrapped the show he got into his black 1988 Mustang and drove home to his West Hollywood condo to settle down in front of the television and watch his daytime competition—Oprah and Phil.

Was it normal, he fretted, to reject the joys of a wife and a family and settle on the joys and frustrations of a television show?

"It's one of my most agonizing thoughts," he admitted. "I guess I can always hook up with a young girl—the time factor isn't as much a consideration for men as it is for women. But I don't see any end in sight.

"I wish I wasn't so *into* what I'm doing. Because you have to have a balance. Some people can do it, have careers and families. They want to do the family thing. And it scares me that I haven't had that desire."

Further, "Is it going to be too late when I decide? Do I want to do it and I'm too stupid and obsessed with my career? I'm totally scared about my future and when it's all going to happen."

It could have happened with Paula Abdul, who hung out with him for several months when the show first started.

About Abdul, he said: "It is—something else. She's what, she's—I consider her—she's, she's really, she's—the perfect woman." He sighed. "She has a career and I have a career and those are, well, relationship busters. . . . I am literally so obsessed with my career that [there's] a terrible sickness to it. . . . Plus I'm a real loner. I couldn't imagine living with somebody. I spend most of my time by myself, alone. That scares me."

Laura B. Randolph got to the heart of the question about Arsenio's love life when she interviewed him for *Ebony* magazine in December 1990. She put it this way:

"Arsenio had his heart broken by an old love who couldn't deal with his Hollywood dreams."

She was, according to Arsenio, a high-school sweetheart of his.

"We went away to the same college," Arsenio told Randolph. "We lived together in college through graduation, and when we got out of college, we moved away and got a job together."

The move from Ohio University to Kent State may have been motivated by Arsenio's desire to be with her. But Arsenio is close-lipped about this period of his life and it is difficult to ascertain the truth.

"This was a six-year relationship that ended because I got in this business," he explained to Randolph for the *Ebony* profile.

"That's not me," this live-in lover of Arsenio's accordingly told him at the time of the permanent split. "You're from Cleveland with dreams of being a star. I'm from Cleveland. Period."

At least, so goes one version of the story of Arsenio's romantic past.

But he is not quite the loner he claims to be. He has had his brief flings, and one minor escapade is worth relating, inasmuch as it fleshes out his real persona.

The tale goes that he once sent a limousine to a woman's house to pick her up for dinner. But this transaction was somewhat unusual. Arsenio had already instructed his date on exactly what to do.

"I told her to put on this particular coat I knew she had, but not to put on anything under it. I had the car pick her up and take her shopping. I told the driver exactly what to do, exactly where to take her, and that what she had on was to be thrown away, and she was to be dressed from head to toe."

Yes, dressed from head to toe, but—in *leather*?

When she had finished her shopping spree in Beverly Hills, the leather lady rode in the limo to The Ivy, a trendy Los Angeles restaurant. There, Arsenio was waiting for her with champagne, flowers, and other goodies. These "other goodies" included a pair of exquisite gold-and-diamond earrings and a matching necklace.

But that wasn't the end. After dinner, they got in the limo and took a long ride.

"In those nice clothes she'd just bought," Arsenio relates with a smile of reminiscence, "we went down on the beach and sat in the sand."

An arresting picture of a more erotic and intimate Arsenio Hall than the one commonly on view.

Meanwhile, rumors about Arsenio's love life continue to fly all over Hollywood and the entertainment business.

"Somewhere I gotta draw the line and say, 'You can't have none of this,'" he told *Playboy* magazine. "And I draw the line when I go home, with my love life and my home life. You can make up all the shit you want: You can say I'm fucking Mary Frann in the car on Tuesdays. Whatever. But the reality—I won't give you any of that."

Maria Shriver brought up the usual question on television one night recently:

"Do you do anything but work? Do you have a girlfriend? Do you have a personal life?"

Arsenio smiled. "Yes. I have a lady who you might say lives with me, because she's never at *her* place. People say I have no life. I say I do."

Life in show business can lead to a number of personal

problems, some of them quite serious. "I know a lot of people in this town and I've seen a lot of them just go crazy. You can get too much into how many houses and how many cars and how many girls. And you can start thinking, Hey, this is happening, let's do some coke. . . . It's real important *not* to get too into being Hollywood and too far away from what you were when you made it."

The drug question was never far from Arsenio's mind. As one of the handful of major black stars on television, he knew that being a role model was a part of what he had undertaken when he got into the late-night talk-show business.

"People are watching me. I'm in the limelight. What I do can become a trend. I can make good times and positive attitudes and a hatred for drug abuse become the in thing because people are watching me.

"I knew when I was a kid, I was affected by what my stars did. Our public figures don't realize the responsibility they have. They are falling to drug addiction and jail sentences left and right."

That was the reason Hall was critical of singer James Brown, who was forced to serve a prison sentence for a car chase involving the police, and featured him in several of his stand-up routines.

"I have no sympathy for people who are blessed, and then break the law," Arsenio said firmly. "I grew up with hope because a man like James Brown succeeded. So I need people like James to realize their responsibility."

And that was the reason Hall was so supportive of Magic Johnson when he came to him and said he wanted to be a leader in the crusade against AIDS. At least Magic Johnson had understood his own importance as a role model and was willing to become a spokesperson in the fight.

It was also on Arsenio's show that Corey Haim, a teenage movie heartthrob, revealed that he was addicted to drugs. In a memorable interview, he told Arsenio that he had looked at himself in the mirror one day after taking a shower and could not recognize the "skin and bones" staring back at him. Arsenio's audience was stunned into silence. This was more than a simple confession. The actor's stricken eyes seemed to hold on to Arsenio, pleading for help. When Haim finally finished his interview and was about to leave, Arsenio gave him a bear hug.

It was because of Arsenio's constant battle against drugs that he was selected early in 1991 to become the first ambassador of the nationwide Drug Abuse Resistance Education (DARE) program. Established in 1983 by the Los Angeles Police Department and the local school districts as an effort to keep kids off drugs, the program sent specially trained police officers to teach schoolchildren how to resist peer pressure, providing information on alcohol and drugs and on alternatives to them.

In his role as first ambassador, Arsenio followed these police officers around the country to speak to and counsel kids on the importance of following their dreams and avoiding the temptations of drugs.

"One of the things I wanted to do with DARE was expose it more to the black community, because in cities like L.A., cops and the black community are not a marriage made in heaven."

He pointed out that most rappers he talked to considered cops the enemy. One told Arsenio, "All my life all the cops ever done to me was cuss at me, mistreated me for the way I'm dressed, screamed at my mother when they were harassing me."

"Here is a situation where I see law enforcement officers doing something positive with the community. It is education from the time when you can first comprehend. That's what DARE does. And it's in all fifty states. I'm trying to align myself with it to bring some attention to it because education and eliminating drugs in our community is the key."

Being in show business, a profession known for its heavy drug usage, Arsenio said that many people assume he uses drugs.

"Women have asked me for cocaine," he said. "Some of them assume that I use cocaine to get up for doing this show every night. People assume that if you're in the business, you've got to do it."

His main message through DARE was this: "I am living proof that being hip and being successful is best achieved by being *drug free*."

As part of his antidrug work, Hall began making a series of public service announcements for television, forming his own company, Arsenio Hall Communications, Ltd., to do so. Made in association with Frank Mancuso, Jr., and Deborah Rosen of Paramount Pictures, Inc., these film clips urged viewers to avoid drugs and alcohol.

One of these that Arsenio made in 1990 featured a sixteen-year-old girl named Nicole who had become a crack addict. A pretty, vivacious young girl, she warned against becoming involved with drugs.

The following year at the time Arsenio was making his new PSA, "Nicole was shot in the head—" Arsenio paused for breath as his eyes brimmed over with tears "—and [was] pushed out of a moving car."

He shook his head. "She had slipped back with the same people, you know, and she started hanging out with them again." He cleared his throat. "So she's dead, you know, and that's—that's what we have to do this for."

Arsenio's battle against drugs was a more immediate and more urgent one than his *most* important and continuing "battle against." That big one was always his primary concern: the battle against racism.

Arsenio is fond of telling a story about his early days when he was opening for Patty LaBelle at Trump Plaza in Atlantic City. Arsenio was going up an escalator and a couple was coming down opposite him.

The woman reached out to Arsenio and said, "Hi!"

The man with her frowned and growled: "What the hell you touching that nigger for!"

"It was one of those things where you didn't even want to fight, it hurt that bad," Arsenio recalls painfully.

The woman told her husband: "Stop! That's Arsenio Hall, the comedian."

"I guess he didn't recognize me in my sweats," Arsenio sighs. "And here's a guy who probably enjoyed my act the night before in the show room, and now I'm a nigger."

Arsenio shakes his head. "You have to remember that, because to some people that's all you are."

Another, longer story might illustrate the point.

"My manager used to handle a female impersonator named Jim Bailey, whom I used to open for," Arsenio says. "He'd be dressing up as Judy Garland, and I'd be going offstage, and I'd knock on his door."

Arsenio would say, "I'll talk to you after the show."

Bailey would respond in falsetto, "Jim's not here. Judy's here."

Arsenio would answer: "Get the fuck out of here, man. If somebody wanted to whip Judy's ass, I'll bet Jim would be here!"

Hearing about this, Jay Leno suggested that Arsenio should do the bit in his act.

"I couldn't," Arsenio pointed out, "because my manager handled Jim and he thought Jim would be mad."

Jay called Arsenio to tell him that he had done the joke one night on the Letterman show, since Arsenio did not want to use the material.

Arsenio explained. "I give him jokes and he gives me jokes."

Later Arsenio *did* do the joke at the Comedy Store. As he was leaving, a white customer came up to Arsenio and confronted him: "You're a fucking asshole to do Jay Leno's joke."

Arsenio was startled. Then he realized what had happened. "It dawned on me that in his mind this joke could not have originated in the mind of a black man. He *had* to have stolen it!"

Jesse Jackson had once suggested that Arsenio could do a great deal to break down television's color barrier. "If it works," Jackson said, "you can be the Jackie Robinson of late-night television," referring to the man who had broken baseball's color barrier.

"All of a sudden," Arsenio said, "I had this awareness of my eighteen-to-twenty-five demographic, and people who wanted to go after that knew that this was the place you had to come. That's the first time I remember saying to myself I might be in the game."

But when the critics got on him for doing this and not doing that, he was hurt—because he was pilloried more than his white peers. He became a target, and he wasn't prepared for that.

"I thought, 'Yeah, I'll be the Jackie Robinson of late night.' What I forgot was that Jackie got booed by a lot of people, you know, and I wasn't ready for that pain."

But he took it anyway, and in the end survived it. In the process he encountered all the pitfalls of racism and reverse racism. One night, he had Michael Jordan on the show and the basketball star said something negative about a Caucasian ballplayer—something that will not be repeated here.

"I found myself ostracized," Arsenio said, "caught between a rock and a hard place—the NAACP saying, 'You're not doing enough'; a white organization saying, 'You're hiring people because they're black.' And I'm in the middle saying, 'Am I making anybody happy?'"

Then he remembered something both Bill Cosby and Jesse Jackson had told him on different occasions:

"Trust your heart. Decide what you're doing is your best effort, and don't let too many people tell you what to do."

Arsenio found himself trusting his heart more than once during the brief but intense Persian Gulf War in 1990–1991.

"I was going to do a joke about what Saddam Hussein would say to his wife on the morning of January fifteenth [the start of the shooting]. When he was going to work I wondered out loud if he would say, 'Honey, don't wait up!'"

On Monday he decided *not* to use the gag. Then on Tuesday, when the staff talked about it, he mulled over the idea again.

"I put a little extra thought into it. Much as I wanted to try to make people laugh in a world that was not always funny, I knew I was doing a joke about war, and that the potential result of war is loss of life—so I'm real, real careful."

Then that night on the show, his guest, Farrah Fawcett, told him that she thought if women ran the world, there wouldn't be any wars.

"She might have a good point," he admitted. "Women deal with problems of greed and power a lot different than men do. I think if our sanctions were pressed a longer time, it would bring Hussein hopefully to his knees."

Eventually, "I chickened out on [the joke]," Arsenio said. "As much as I believe our country should function from a position of strength, what's going on now is not worth bloodshed. I place a lot of value on life."

When the 1991 fall season approached, Hall had become an established show-business personality—one of a trio of black actor/comics composed of Bill Cosby, Eddie Murphy, and Arsenio Hall. He had established his show as more than a contender; it was a success. He was going into his third fall season.

And it was time for a more obvious, more dramatic change in *looks*. Scott Julian, a hair stylist, had sent him a drawing of a new hairstyle to take the place of the squared-off hip-hop style that had gained Arsenio the sobriquet "trapezoid head," "flat top," and other unmentionable names.

"I was so excited about the drawing this guy brought me that I said, 'Let's do it for the MTV awards, so I can be criticized internationally.'"

And so the old squared-off hip-hop Arsenio became a more moderately styled celebrity in September 1991.

"In the ghetto," Arsenio said, "it would be termed 'fried, dyed, and kicked in the side.' It's longer on top," he explained, and the sides were nearly nude. "Instead of the dramatic hard corners and flat top, it has a reckless lean to it, a Chicago kind of lean."

The response, Arsenio said, was 90 percent positive. "I'm at that stage of life when you can't go to the basket as quick. When a woman told me I looked younger, I sent Scott another check!"

What Arsenio was *really* doing was bringing himself more into the mainstream. He had played a freaky oddball role to gain attention, and he was now taking another direction to consolidate the power that was now his.

There was in Arsenio Hall's demeanor a new *inner* power. He had a certain daring about him. The way he carried himself, the way he walked, and talked, the way he took hold of a situation, all these exuded confidence. His manner suggested his ability to unleash that inner power. It was the greatest aphrodisiac of all; it was the greatest charisma a man could have.

17

Street-Smart Schmoozer

In spite of Arsenio Hall's rapid transformation into a big-time celebrity, the key to his success as a late-night talk-show host is his remarkable ability as a stand-up comic and *not* his talent for interviewing or for engaging guests in riveting conversation. He had begun as a comic and continued to flourish as a comic because of his verbal thrusts and miming expertise. His aura of celebrity was frosting on the cake.

And he liked to keep close tabs on his jokes because he knew his humor was what made him what he was. "I don't think I've ever done a joke I didn't have a hand in writing," he told one interviewer.

Despite his crossover image as a talented trend-setter for the young and style-setter for the more mature, which made him more a generalist than a specialist, his humor was still just a bit *over* the line of traditional taste, a bit further out than what might be considered middle ground for the average viewer. This gave it a little spice to intrigue middle America.

One critic assessed it as "low-key observational humor," which was "spiked with naughty sex jokes and references, often irreverent, to black culture and its stars." Another pointed out that his humor was basically sexual innuendo or plays on four-letter words. Still another called it a combination of "street smarts" and "Vegas schmooze."

No less an expert than television's arbiter of pop psychology, Dr. Joyce Brothers, once said that the public *needs* humor to survive, humor more or less of the type associated with Arsenio Hall (although she did not mention him). European jokes, Dr. Brothers found, are generally concerned with excrement—bathroom humor—while most American dirty jokes are based on two elements: sexuality and race. Example:

> JACKIE MASON (*to his mother*): I've fallen in love.
> MRS. MASON: With a nice Jewish girl?
> MASON: Ma, she's a Gentile.
> MRS. MASON: Why couldn't you be gay like everybody else?

"Laughter diverts a person's mind from his ills," she wrote in *TV Guide*. "It offers respite from pain and gloom, rather like a mini-vacation. It also lowers muscle tension, which can, in itself, reduce pain, lower blood pressure and alleviate stress." She mentioned a French physician, Henri de Mondeville, who paid storytellers to amuse his postoperative patients for the relaxing effect of laughter, which helped the healing process.

The typical "dirty joke" that Arsenio carefully crafted into his nightly stand-up monologue fitted meticulously into Dr. Brothers's profile of basic American humor.

Arsenio knew the importance of humor in his success. He also knew that now that he had made it to a very high level, he had to keep himself in trim. And that meant that he could never bask in the illusory warmth of success, but must keep close tabs day by day on his effectiveness as a humorist by studying his own performance and continuing to hone it.

His stand-ups after a year and a half had improved immeasurably. And it was on his stand-ups that he—quite accurately—based his own success.

An informal analysis of his jokes breaks them into six general categories:

- Scatological and bathroom humor, usually dealing with calls of nature and so on;
- Sexual jokes: anatomical words, plays on four-letter words, sexual innuendo;
- Nonsensical rap, sending up offbeat newspaper items;
- Basic name-drop humor, citing familiar media targets;
- Witty references to black cultural figures;
- Straightforward well-told anecdotes of a very general nature.

The typical bathroom joke mentioned by Joyce Brothers accounts for a number of Arsenio Hall's monologues. He came up with a prototypical example a few months after he started his own show.

"Geez! Did you see the paper today?" he asked his audience unbelievingly. "Some poor folks in California had a twenty-four-foot boa constrictor removed from their *toilet*!" Pause. "From their *toilet*!" he repeated. The audience began laughing.

"Can you imagine?" Arsenio went on. "Someone be sittin' there, mindin' his own business, answerin' nature's call when a *snake* starts coming up from below!"

A bit of mugging, and then he sucked in his cheeks and held his breath.

"Oh, I'd hold it in *forever* if I thought there was a snake down there. Ol' Mother Nature wouldn't get nuthin' outta me. No way, no how. And I mean FOREVER!"

The second category consisted of sexual innuendo or jokes in some instances based wholly on the mention and/ or recitation of a play on a four-letter word.

For example, during the recent Iraq-Kuwait troubles, after Iraq had invaded Kuwait, Arsenio quoted a newspaper story in which Saddam Hussein had warned the Western powers that anyone who tried to cross the border into Iraq would have his eyes plucked out by Iraqi troops.

Letting that sink in, he swaggered a bit, leaning into the camera as if he were President Bush telling Hussein to read his lips: "Pluck you!" Laughter. Arsenio repeated the phrase with a slightly different intonation and said it a third time.

He then turned to the audience and led them in a chant of the same phrase as if he were a high-school cheerleader.

By getting them to join in the ritual, he afforded them the thrill of shouting out an alternative to a familiar forbidden four-letter word.

The third category of jokes that Arsenio likes to use involved nonsensical things reported in the newspapers. "Since I've started doing this show," Arsenio announced one night, "I've told you about a lot of *strange* things. I always look in the paper to try to find weird stuff to tell you about. And I always seem to be able to find it!"

He was talking about the stories that usually reinforce the often-quoted aphorism that "truth is stranger than fiction." Will Rogers got great mileage years ago with his statement: "All I know is what I read in the papers." In Arsenio Hall's hands, as in Will Rogers's, the material is usually turned into a kind of "politically correct" statement.

"Ah, what's in the news today?" he began one night. "A preacher in Illinois is going to jail because he was selling cocaine to people in his church."

Arsenio did not need to wait for the laughter. It came

instantly. Obviously, in the real world, things were far more topsy-turvy than in the world we *think* we live in, where church is a place to worship.

"The interesting thing is," Arsenio continued, his eyes gleaming, "I wonder if this is a Baptist church."

More laughter. Arsenio waited the proper moment, and then went on.

"'Cause my church is already very *high-spirited*, very *exciting*. I would hate to see the people in the congregation on cocaine."

More laughter. He did not let it drop there, but went on into an imaginative harangue about drugs and the ministry. But the humor was always there—humor with a sharp, dangerous edge to it. The joke was a risky one because Arsenio had already made a number of commercials against drugs. But taking an issue that was risky was part of his style.

It was *expected* of him.

He never let his audience down.

Another night he mentioned a news item about digging up the body of President Zachary Taylor to find out if he had been poisoned as it had been rumored. Then he wondered aloud what would happen if they found out that he had been poisoned. Were they going to dig up the perpetrator and arrest him?

Zany stuff right out of the newspapers.

The fourth category of Arsenio's humor involved the use of basic target names in the news—names that always seemed to get a laugh, no matter what the contest. Dan Quayle. John Sununu. Elvis Presley.

One evening he started spinning a yarn about driving through downtown Cleveland on his way out to the studio in Hollywood—he had a running gag that he commuted from Cleveland every day to do his show—and a homeless guy came up and started cleaning his windshield.

Arsenio pretended not to notice him in the hope that

he could simply drive on and forget about paying for the service. But the homeless guy finished and rapped on the window.

"May I have a dollar?"

Without looking, Arsenio reached in his pocket and handed a dollar out.

Suddenly the homeless guy did a double-take and said: "Arsenio Hall?"

Arsenio turned and stared out at the man. Short pause. "Donald Trump?"

That was just after Donald Trump's empire had begun to topple and he had been forced to recoup with the sale of one building or business after another. He had abruptly become the world's richest pauper—or most impoverished billionaire.

The structure of the Arsenio Hall anecdote is the perfect example of how to build a story and top it off with the simple utterance of a well-known target name.

The fifth category of Arsenio Hall's jokes concerns references to black culture and its heroes and villains.

At one of his stand-ups, Arsenio announced that the godfather of soul music, James Brown, had been incarcerated in a South Carolina prison.

"Damn, James Brown is the homecoming queen of Cellblock H," he said. "Can't you just see it?"

He went into his big male macho voice, lowering it two octaves. "James—you my *bitch* now!"

At another time Arsenio mentioned Ralph Abernathy's book about Martin Luther King, Jr. Abernathy had alleged in the book a number of the Reverend King's sexual escapades and had denigrated them.

"He's just jealous!" said Arsenio. "Probably hasn't been with three women in his life!" He concluded: "Martin's still my hero. Right on!"

Arsenio also used straight anecdotes that did not fit into the previous, more specific categories. His straight anecdote might unwind like a short story by someone like O. Henry—up to and including the trick ending.

One night he told about purchasing a new car alarm to protect his automobile from thieves. The only trouble with it was that it kept going off for no reason at all. The neighbors grew to hate it—and hated him for buying it. Sure enough, the night before, at four in the morning, the alarm went off, waking him up.

From the window he could see somebody in a ski mask beside his car. Then, before he could get into his bathrobe, a neighbor down the street came running up and grabbed the man in the mask. Then from across the street and everywhere other neighbors rushed up and began beating the would-be thief.

By that time, Arsenio was downstairs and running over to find the would-be thief on the ground, unconscious, bleeding, and terribly injured. Arsenio was touched that his neighbors had been so quick to try to stop the thief. What could he do but thank them?—which he did.

The neighbors looked down at the unconscious man in the ski mask, and then up at Arsenio. One of them said:

"We thought that was *you!*"

Arsenio Hall has always been a student of humor—using it, seeing how it plays, analyzing what makes people laugh, what makes them clam up, what makes people annoyed. Mostly he studies himself.

"People think I'm the black Alan Alda," he said. "When you see me clean-shaven and with a suit on, I think you see something very commercial and brown bread. And no matter what I did, likability always got me over.

"People do humor based on who they are and where they're from," he went on. "Sometimes there's a Bill Cosby, who is black, and his humor is more generic."

When Cosby was starting out, he used to categorize the people in his sketches as white people, black people. A friend once told him: "If you weren't black, you wouldn't have an act." That got to Cosby. He took the remark to heart.

"Ever since," Arsenio said, "he always tried to do comedy where there was absolutely no reference to color." But few people emulated Cosby. "I think everybody's looking for a unique position, hook, or vantage point," Arsenio said. "They're trying to find out 'Who am I?' and 'What do I know the most about?'"

Arsenio took Cosby's lesson to heart early on. He thought of his humor as universal, yet there were issues he had to do battle with. One involved the use of the word *nigger*.

"I got a friend, Paul Mooney, who drives me insane because every other word [he uses] is 'nigger.' First of all, the word gets on my nerves. I never use it as a stand-up comic. If I was *playing* a character who used that word, that's fine, but as Arsenio I'm very uncomfortable with the word. I don't even use it with brothers.

"I've talked to two comedians about that—Paul Mooney and Dick Gregory—and they both have the same philosophy. Dick said the word was created as a weapon against black people. He said by using the word, what he does in essence is take the weapon away, make it satirical, make it a joke and it's no longer a detriment. And I don't buy that."

Arsenio once confessed that he always tended to be a little too serious about comedy.

"One of the first jokes I ever wrote was, 'My name is Arsenio. That's a very unique name for a black man. In Greek it means Leroy.' There was a night when some white people laughed too hard for me. And it was like: You all enjoyed that *too* much. Thank you. Good night.

"They're laughing because you touched that racist bone that they can't fuck with because they might get their ass beat. But since you did it for them, thank goodness—because I love that kind of stuff and I think y'all *are* named Leroy anyway."

Comedy was always the most important thing in the life of Arsenio Hall.

"It makes you conscious of what you do, because just making money [entertaining] isn't enough. There's a pride thing there. I don't do anything that I don't want to come back on me later. You have to think about what you're doing, think about the ramifications of your own— uh—mess."

18

Life After Carson

The television broadcasting world was shaken in early June 1991 with an earthquake of unprecedented proportions. The temblor occurred when NBC-TV announced officially that Johnny Carson, the king of late-night TV, would be abdicating his throne on May 22, 1992.

That put up for grabs the one prime slice of the television terrain that had been solidly entrenched for at least thirty years. The uproar that followed the announcement was stunning.

Not that Carson's position had never before been threatened. It had been—many times. But in the case of the major assailants—from Joey Bishop and Alan Thicke to Joan Rivers and Pat Sajak—all had been brushed off by Carson like flies off a horse's back with a well-aimed flick of the tail.

The question that arose immediately was elemental: Who would take Carson's place?

The heir apparent had been announced in almost the same breath as Carson's abdication had been made public.

But *that* news made much less of an impression. Jay Leno, NBC-TV said, would take Carson's place.

But what about David Letterman, the NBC-TV talk-show host who followed Johnny Carson on late-night TV? Had he not been anointed earlier as Carson's successor? And was it not true that Letterman was Johnny Carson's hand-picked and favored candidate?

In fact, Carson was reportedly "surprised" at the Leno story. "He's acutely embarrassed," one source told *TV Guide*. No one had even *told* Carson who had been selected to replace him!

An NBC-TV insider added: "Many people think Letterman is much better at interviews and that Leno is just a comedian. And by picking Leno over Letterman, NBC didn't just shoot itself in the foot—it shot itself in the belly."

Letterman was rumored to have been livid at being passed over by the network bosses. Perhaps. But after he got his own show on NBC-TV at 12:30 A.M., he had more or less vanished from the 11:30, late prime-time scene to settle himself comfortably into the post-midnight world, where he had begun to build up a tight little clique of admirers. It was Jay Leno who had become the most available and permanent guest host.

And, on May 25, 1992, he took over *The Tonight Show* on NBC. The question then became not who would replace Carson (who was, of course, irreplaceable), but how long would Leno last in the spot? For a while he held his own. By September 1992 he was still number one in the late-night sweepstakes. But it was obvious that things might change in the future. The late-night audience was as fickle as any other audience. Who would become the *real* leader?

The battlefield was far from deserted. Leno was, of course, he who had the proper papers and the shoulder tap of the network. It was up to time to prove him or disapprove of him.

*   *   *

And there was David Letterman, the passed-over former favorite. Since the initial blow, Letterman was rumored to have been "talking" to potential employers all
over the place. His main targets were syndicators of talk
shows. After all, that was where the big money—and the
clout—was. With Mike Ovitz, a Hollywood powerhouse
agent to pave the way for him, Letterman consulted CBS,
Paramount, King World, and—especially—ABC. Would he
make a move? And if he did, when would he do so? His
contract with NBC would expire in April 1993. Was that
the pivotal moment? Stay tuned.

Ted Koppel had worked for ten years on ABC-TV's
Nightline at 11:30, catering to and developing an audience
interested in news, current events, and politics, rather than
jokes and celebrity tittle-tattle. In August 1992, he was
number two behind Leno in late-night TV. Now, if Letterman chose to go to ABC-TV, would Letterman move
into the 11:30 slot to face Jay Leno—thus pushing Koppel
ahead to 12:30—or would he opt to follow Koppel at
12:00? And if whatever happened was displeasing to Koppel, what would Koppel do? He *was* number two.

On September 14, 1992, Whoopi Goldberg, fresh from
her role in the summer sleeper film hit *Sister Act,* debuted
in a syndicated nightly half-hour talk show that had been
in the discussion stage for months. Each segment featured
one guest only, with subjects ranging from entertainment
to politics, with no rigidly set parameters.

"This is not a show about newsmakers," the star said. "It's
about conversing." *TV Guide* described *The Whoopi Goldberg Show* as a "patchwork of network-affiliated and independent stations across the country"—a kind of Arsenio
Hall mockup.

The set was a spacious, well-appointed apartment,

with a remote piano player supplying incidental melody. But no audience. No desk. No stand-up monologue. Interviewer and interviewee switched places on the show: Whoopi was on the left, the guest on the right—the mirror opposite of most all other talk shows. "I'm a lefty. I always sit on the left," she noted.

She was reportedly being paid five million by Genesis Entertainment. In the New York market, the show aired at 11 P.M. every night on Channel 9, a perfect lead-in for the Arsenio Hall show at 11:30. Saturday and Sunday nights reprised two of the week's best at 10:30 P.M. Openers the first week included Elizabeth Taylor and *Cheers'* Ted Danson, plus Elton John, Robin Williams, and, for added dimension, white supremacist Tom Metzger.

For some time Chevy Chase, at one time a leading contender for the job of replacing Johnny Carson on *The Tonight Show,* had been dickering with the Fox network for a slot in the late-night time frame. Chase, of course, was known primarily as an actor—not a conversationalist, an interviewer, or even a host.

It was Lucie Salhany at Fox—she was formerly president of Paramount Domestic TV when the Arsenio Hall show was incubated—who spearheaded the talk with Chevy Chase. The general format under consideration was one that depended a great deal on skits and comedy—more like the spots on the Carson show in which he played various roles.

As Chase himself put it: "Basically, it will be an exact copy of David Letterman without the gap between his teeth."

It would be Fox's first venture into night-time talk since their disastrous adventure with *The Wilton North Report* back in 1987–1988.

If there was a problem with Chase, it was whether or not he could keep his mouth shut and *listen.* For an actor, listening is the hardest thing in the world to do. To talk is the easiest. Would he be controlled enough to produce a conversation and not a monologue?

Proposed debut: September 1993.

There were a number of also-rans, one of whom was Jonathon Brandmeier, an amiable Chicago disk jockey with almost as unpronounceable a name as Arnold Schwarzenegger—but had that hurt *him* at the box office? Brandmeier, called "Johnny B" on the air, promised more than just a lot of sit-down gab.

"With so many talk shows, I'd be crazy to try and compete" on a level of talk, talk, and more talk, he said. The idea would be to feature himself in zany situations, getting away from the set and maybe doing a street scene with the camera crew now and then.

And there was Arsenio Hall, who had begun his late-night life in January 1989 in a head-to-head contest with Pat Sajak for the late-night sweepstakes—a contest that Hall had won hands down when Sajak's show was canceled in April 1990, a year and three months after it had started. In August 1992 he was number three in late-night talk.

It would take a fortune-teller to determine which of these seven probable candidates would in the end win out, if indeed any of them managed to generate staying power after debuting.

Two of those favored seven seemed to be emerging as viable possibilities to replace Carson at the top.

One was Jay Leno.

The other was Arsenio Hall.

Two years ago one might well have asked: "*Who* Hall?" But that had all changed. Arsenio was now as well known a one-name celebrity as Madonna or Cher.

Why did anyone care who was at the top of the

heap—especially an esoteric heap with as many weirdos and oddballs as the late-night talk-show roster held? Because he who rules the roost of late-night talk brings in the most bucks in revenue. The profits in late-night broadcasting are astronomical; they balance out the deadbeats and the sick turkeys strewn all over the graveyard of prime-time TV.

"The comedy-talk shows are not expensive to produce," Rick Ludwin, senior vice president of late-night programming for NBC-TV, pointed out. "You have a regular format that uses the same set every night. Once you amortize those fixed costs, you can make a lot of money in a hurry."

There were more reasons than simply the quick-buck turnaround. For example, for the last few years two competitors have been eating into the profits of prime-time television: cable television's wide-ranging accessibility and the rising popularity of VCR rentals of movies. Thus late-night TV has become a fiercely competitive arena.

Obviously the network that controlled the night-time talk-show territory was going to be the network able to generate the most income from its advertising and thus pay for its prime-time mistakes more easily.

And it was in the late-night talk-show area that television had always been its most innovative. The talk show—called a "chat show" on British television—was one of the most original developments in broadcasting since television sprang from radio.

Of course radio had its talk shows as well, low-keyed conversations rather than give-and-take interviews. For example, Ed and Pegeen Fitzgerald had chatted with each other and interviewed celebrities of all kinds in a morning radio slot. So had Tex McCrary and Jinx Falkenberg. So had many others.

Yet when that kind of easygoing conversation moved from radio to television, it struck a veritable gold mine.

Celebrities are generally even more charismatic visually than verbally. Now that the audience could *see* as well as hear them, they became irresistible. It was that extra dimension—sight as well as sound—that established one of TV's most popular forms.

In fact, the talk-show format was a surprisingly compelling development from the beginning. In the 1950s, television was just getting started. There were three networks—mostly simple spin-offs from the radio nets—and all three ran old motion pictures after prime time was through. One network even called the program of old movies shown after midnight *The Late Late Show*. "Late late" meant black-and-white motion pictures. By 11:00 P.M., the moguls in the broadcasting towers decreed in their wisdom, all honest people were in bed.

The bigwigs at NBC-TV in New York got a bright idea. Movies, they felt, were just putting people to sleep. How about inventing some kind of live entertainment to keep people awake and sell them things? Why not put the spotlight of TV on, say, a comic from burlesque days and let him perform on the cheap? He could even read the commercials like an old-fashioned pitchman!

And so it was that in May 1950 NBC-TV in New York introduced a show strictly for insomniacs called *Broadway Open House*. It came on every weeknight at eleven. Actually, it was two shows. The host for Tuesday, Thursday, and Friday was Jerry Lester, an old vaudevillian; the host for Monday and Wednesday was Morey Amsterdam, a decade before he made his big breakthrough as comedy writer Maurice "Buddy" Sorrell in 1961 on *The Dick Van Dyke Show*.

The big hit of *Broadway Open House* was neither Lester nor Amsterdam, but a female foil named Dagmar, hired one night by Lester to read wacky poems in the style of a poor man's Gracie Allen. The idea was to hype up the somewhat uneven show. She was a towering clotheshorse, abundantly endowed, and tastelessly funny in a zingy way. Her humor was elemental at best, much of it ad-libbed—and a lot of it right on the borderline of what would have been considered obscene in that unenlightened era.

Guests in show business flocked to the late-night scene for conversation with pipsqueak Lester, gargantuan Dagmar, and crazy Amsterdam. Who cared if celebrities plugged their movies, their plays, their television shows? The talk thing was reviving conversation, and insomniac America seemed to be developing a brand new culture.

And America listened—to the talkers and, more importantly for the future of talk shows, to the commercials.

The ratings rose, and this exhilarated the NBC-TV accountants, who had had little to cheer about in their late-night entries. It was widely held that talk shows might become television's most prolific makers of profit. Showbiz stars, even those paid inflated rates for their work, were happy to work for scale—or less—to plug themselves.

Plus which, you could get away with jokes late at night that you couldn't earlier in the evening when the kids were monopolizing the TV set.

In the end Lester got sick of Dagmar's unexpected popularity, felt it was robbing him of his image, and tried to get rid of her. But the brass saw her as strength. Soon she was making almost as much money as he was. Lester hired another female foil to do her in, but that ploy failed. He learned to his sorrow that, in the manner of Dr. Frankenstein, he had created a monster who was threatening to destroy him. In the end it did. Lester quit *Broadway Open House.* Amsterdam had already left. When Lester quit, the show sank into oblivion.

It was Steve Allen who finally rescued the eleven o'clock slot with a somewhat different format in 1953. This program was dubbed *The Tonight Show.* At the time Allen became host, it was still a local New York show, but fifteen months later, in 1954, it went network, with Allen continuing in the top slot.

He pioneered late-night conversation for several years, alternating with Ernie Kovacs as host. Allen quit in 1957, at which time the show was rechristened *Tonight! America After Dark,* with Jack Lescouli for a while and then Al "Jazzbo" Collins, but it was floundering in this format.

In July 1957 Jack Paar took over, and the show became *The Jack Paar Show.* He served almost five years and left in 1962, when the show returned to its original network title, *The Tonight Show.* A number of announcers hosted it then, Hugh Downs, Jack Haskell, and Ed Herlihy among them. But this jerry-rigged version didn't last long either.

Johnny Carson became host in October 1962—and the rest, of course, is television history. Carson was responsible for laying down the rules for late-night talk-show television in the ensuing years.

When he took over, the show had moved from the 11:00 slot to 11:15 to allow the local stations on the NBC-TV network to broadcast late-breaking news. Carson felt that the quarter-hour time was an odd one to start a show. In 1965 he flatly refused to appear at 11:15 and came on at 11:30. Ed McMahon and Skitch Henderson, the leader of the band at the time, carried the show at 11:15. Carson made his point: that a lot of local stations had stretched their late news to a half hour, and thus a monologue at 11:15 would be lost to many viewers. In January 1967, the show shifted to its present starting time of 11:30.

Also, when Carson took over, the show was broadcast from New York, but he felt that the pool of entertainment talent was larger in Hollywood, and he agitated for a shift to the West Coast. In May 1972 the entire show pulled up stakes in New York and moved to Burbank, California.

Carson established another precedent. In those days, the show was taped a day ahead of broadcast time. Carson was aware that quick-breaking news could make his monologues stale overnight. He opted to tape each show on the afternoon of its nightly broadcast—and that schedule has been maintained to this day.

It was the combination of Paar and Carson, with some flashbacks to Allen, that coalesced the format—a format that deliberately avoided controversy in favor of the vacuous banter of recognizable celebrities.

A TV analyst named Arthur Asa Berger of San Francisco State University commented on the new talk-show craze: "With their super-rich diet of strong, assertive celebrities, talk shows are spreading the notion that to be ordinary is to be irrevelant. Without realizing it, the silent, passive nobodies may be adopting these flashy individuals as role models."

Mike Douglas and Merv Griffin perpetuated this easy style of conversation in the daytime and made it ever smoother and blander. Carson was, of course, the prototype of slick. He once wisecracked that his show was "NBC's answer to foreplay."

Douglas and Griffin were not alone. Dick Cavett, the darling of the intellectuals, soon hosted a heady competitive show on ABC-TV and later on public television. There one could watch stodgy Ivy League types smirking and conversing with all the vapid dynamism of characters loosed from a Chekhov play. Later on, Phil Donahue worked his way into the arena, and shortly after him, Oprah Winfrey—not only a woman, but a black woman at that!

But there was another subgenre of late-night show that was succeeding as well. Mike Wallace, who initiated it in 1956, invented and perfected it almost single-handedly. It was the inquisitorial style of interview, a show featuring a guest (victim?) and host (public prosecutor?). It was a verbal third degree on the small screen. Wallace's show was called *Night Beat.* One wag suggested it be renamed *Night Beating.*

While Phil Donahue added Wallace's hatchet-in-hand

style to his interviews, he did not do it with the same verve or glee. And most of Donahue's attacks were friendly ones, simply mounted for information.

It was Morton Downey, Jr., who became the bête noire of the interview game, but he was syndicated for only a short time in the late 1980s. His attacks and snide remarks finally got on the nerves not only of viewers but account executives as well, and he vanished from view.

Which direction will late-night talk go with Carson out of the saddle? Will it become more sleek and defensive, the way it was before Carson added just a bit of zest and tongue-in-cheek cynicism to the genre? Or will it go further and further into the stratosphere of news manipulation and become the format of front-page headlines?

Or will it become nothing more than a kind of extended *Saturday Night Live,* with parodies, satires, and gags pricking holes in the usual targets? Will the humor become even more politically correct than it was during Carson's regime, or will it venture into new fields and more dangerous pastures?

Jay Leno has continued much in the same manner as his mentor. However, he did drop Ed McMahon and Doc Severinsen. There had been talk that he might use *Saturday Night Live*'s Dana Carvey, or even Jan Hooks, who had recently joined *Designing Women,* but it was just that—talk.

He also dropped the character sketches that Carson was famous for: Carnac the Magnificent, Aunt Blabby, the Great Carsoni, Faharishi, Floyd R. Turbo, and Father Time.

As for his interviewing technique, he tended toward the bland. Even his jokes were toned down. "I don't do wife jokes and I don't do Dolly Parton jokes."

Leno inherited a problem. NBC-TV had been fully independent. Now, however, it was owned by the huge General Electric conglomerate. The books showed that

Carson's hour alone took in about $100 million a year for
NBC-TV in commercials. Of course, Carson's salary was
about $25 million a year. Leno's was some $3 million. The
bottom line was money. The future would depend on
Leno's ability to keep the ratings alive—on that and on that
alone.

He had been selected over David Letterman, it was
said, because *his* Q Rating—Quotient of Recognition (it's
really a likability factor)—was at least eight points higher
than Letterman's, and even slightly higher than Johnny
Carson's. But there was yet another factor at work in
NBC's zeroing in on Leno.

CBS-TV had quite aggressively flirted with Leno before he signed with NBC-TV. The rival network had almost
won him over, it was said; money *did* talk loud and clear.
But in the end, Leno decided to stick it out with NBC-TV
because of the fact that he was comfortable there and was
recognized as part of the Carson tradition.

"It wasn't that hard a choice [to select Leno over Let-
terman]," one late-night producer said. "Leno is more
mainstream. David has more a niche program, a cult
program."

Anyway, "No promises were ever made that [Let-
terman] would be offered the Carson job."

The one to watch, of course, was Arsenio Hall.

The New York Times's John J. O'Connor wrote that
in consideration of the sweepstakes to come, Hall was the
contender who had earned special consideration—and went
on to detail the pluses and minuses of his persona.

The minuses mostly concerned lack of polish and
Hall's hyperactivity on the set:

• The woof-woof antics he used to arouse his audiences were getting tired and seemed redundant, considering the general spirit of his youthful viewers
without being deliberately hyped up.

- The embarrassed and addled manner in which he frequently handled his monologue material when he realized that the stuff was not up to scratch was off-putting, as was his sophomoric way of giggling at his own jokes.
- Although O'Connor did not mention it, Arsenio sometimes let his interviews meander thoughtlessly into bad taste.

For the most part, though, Arsenio Hall had a lot of pluses, according to O'Connor, which included:

- The ability to go one on one with a guest that he himself liked and was interested in; no one in the late-night arena could come close to his capacity for inspiring guests to open up about themselves the way he could when he had a guest who was on his special wavelength.
- The fact that his show was probably the most racially integrated of all talk shows, with guests spanning a broad range from Ed Bradley of *60 Minutes* through Spike Lee to Whoopi Goldberg and from Tom Selleck and Madonna through Mel Gibson and Harrison Ford, was a major plus.
- His talent at mimicry in playing various roles, especially when his material might be a bit below par, paid off dividends. O'Connor particularly mentioned Arsenio's indebtedness to Flip Wilson, whose Geraldine and heavy-handed street-macho male he continually mimicked.
- His ability to keep the guests in line so that they neither grew bored nor stepped out of control showed finesse.
- His penchant for slipping in his own line of activism with comments about blacks and whites, and his ability to remain politically correct even when some of

his guests might try to draw him into other areas, were basic and most viable assets.

Thus Arsenio Hall appeared to be the man who was smiling the most broadly at the departure of Johnny Carson. It would be an uphill battle to unseat the favorite, who was already ahead of him by points and by being on the inside. But Arsenio had been in this kind of joust before.

A popularity poll taken by *Time* magazine in August 1991 found Arsenio Hall at the top of the heap when it came to late-night talk-show hosts. He took 32 percent of the vote as "favorite gabfest host" on late-night TV.

David Letterman came in second, with 23 percent. Jay Leno finished third with 20 percent. The remaining 25 percent was split among others.

On *First Person*, November 12, 1991, Maria Shriver talked about what would happen after Carson retired.

"While [Arsenio] Hall doesn't want to appear competitive with his boyhood idol, Johnny Carson," she noted, "he says that will all change when the king of late night retires on May 22. After that it's all-out war."

Arsenio agreed. "I have a certain kind of respect for Johnny Carson. When he's gone, the word *respect* will only come out of Aretha's mouth."

"So it's going to be different?" Shriver asked.

"It's hardball then."

19
Polishing the Image

Arsenio Hall's ambition was always on the front burner. It had never really cooled down, even with the phenomenal success of his late-night talk show. He had a contract to make four motion pictures. He was obligated to produce three Arsenio Hall specials for television. And he had other irons in the fire as well.

It was after the success of *The Arsenio Hall Show*—it climbed steadily during its first year to gain the number-two late-night spot just behind Johnny Carson (if one does not count Ted Koppel's more serious interview show)—that Arsenio and his production company at Paramount began looking around for other late-night fields to conquer.

And they found one.

From the time she was seven years old in Hollywood, Nia Peeples had studied dancing, per her father's wishes. Her father, Robert Peeples, was a Scotsman, and her mother, Elizabeth, was Filipino. Nia grew up as exotic-looking as she was supple and talented in dancing. Fated to be a leader among her many friends, Nia simply relaxed and enjoyed her early fame.

"I could never go to a dance and just dance," she told *People* magazine. "I had to be running the damned thing."

Nia Peeples graduated from West Covina High School in Los Angeles with straight A's, tried UCLA for one semester, and went on to greater things by returning to high school, in this case the High School of the Performing Arts on the television program titled *Fame*. There she played the sexy song-and-dance virtuoso Nicole Chapman from 1984 through 1987.

After Nicole was killed off in 1987, Nia scored a hit with the title track for a 1988 debut album, *Nothin' but Trouble*. She married her coproducer, Howard Hewett, and went on in 1987 to cohost *Top of the Pops* for CBS-TV for one season and to host MTV's *Street Scene*.

Arsenio met Peeples at a party late in 1990, was impressed by her talent and looks, and began gestating an idea that turned out to be a production story all of its own.

For some time he had been looking for a show that might link up with his own—a kind of extension of the party idea that was the basis of his show. Perhaps, he thought, it could be a kind of "après-party" party. And that was the idea that finally jelled after Peeples came on the scene.

The show was titled *The Party Machine with Nia Peeples*. As Arsenio put it to the publicity people who began to spread the word about the show, "Whenever I go out, people always ask, 'Where's the party?'"

Answer: "Stay tuned."

The *Machine,* Arsenio said, will "always be the show for people who want the party to continue and don't want to hear any more talking." It would follow the *Arsenio Hall Show,* profiting from that show's high lead-in ratings.

"Arsenio's audience doesn't sleep," Peeples said. "I can't watch his show and get tired. I sit there and feel like I'm in his home."

Besides—who wants to keep talking after midnight? That's the time for action!

She had no illusions about her ability to carry the show. "I was kind of leery at first," she said, discussing Arsenio's idea. "I don't want to be Arsenio Hall. I'm not a stand-up comedian."

"I see Nia as the smartest, most versatile, gorgeous woman in her category, and I know them all," Arsenio retorted. "She dances, she sings, she acts, she's a mother, and you're looking at the face of an angel."

Nevertheless, with all the hooplah and high hopes, *Party Machine with Nia Peeples* was a ratings flop early in 1991 and was canceled after a few futile months of syndication.

The failure of this production venture was not good news to Arsenio Hall. What made the disaster harder to sustain was the fact that the ratings of his own show had begun to plummet at the same time.

In January 1989, *The Arsenio Hall Show* premiered on 141 stations with fairly negative reviews from the print medium. However, after a faltering beginning, the show began to rise slowly and then with quickening vigor. By the start of 1991 it was airing on 175 stations.

However, in 1991, when the Persian Gulf War suddenly flared up, the audience for *The Arsenio Hall Show* simply tuned out and tuned in cable and news channels. The war was short-lived, and when it was over the audience came back strongly. So strongly that when Magic Johnson appeared to speak about AIDS, nine million households—the largest audience Arsenio Hall had ever had—tuned in.

But no one can count on a Magic Johnson to rescue a program on a regular basis. Perhaps it was time for Arsenio to take stock of the strengths and weaknesses of his three-year-old show—especially with the looming abdication of the late-night throne by Johnny Carson.

And so it was in the late months of 1991 that Arsenio Hall hired a research company to make a study of his fans.

The idea was to discover what his audience liked and what it did not like. How was the overall show viewed? How did the music play? How did the monologues go? How were the interviews perceived?

Frank Magid and Associates, the research firm, did an in-depth survey and brought the findings back to Paramount and Arsenio.

"They did focus groups," Arsenio told the *Los Angeles Times*, "and we sat behind mirrors, and Paramount executives flew into some cities to listen to people."

The findings were carefully studied and analyzed.

"One of the most interesting things that came out of it was that fans thought if my competitors and I talked to the same guests, I would get more out of them."

Arsenio had a good chuckle about *that* finding.

"So all the things that the critics were saying about me, fans were in the total opposite direction."

There were other events in the offing that did not please Arsenio and his crew. Although Jay Leno seemed to be settling down comfortably in the groove at *The Tonight Show* with no indication that he would try breaking new ground, there was some excitement when *The Dennis Miller Show* debuted late in January 1992. A syndicated show, it got off to a great start—especially with the critics.

Touted by some as the "perfect postmodernist talk-show host," Miller in the beginning was making some inroads into the late-night crowd. Somewhere on the way out in space toward David Letterman in concept and choice of material, the Miller show was getting noticed.

Kit Boss wrote in the *Seattle Times* about the oddball subjects he covered in his shows:

- A reference to a Spanish film director who founded surrealist cinema.
- References to pop songs by Bobby Goldsboro, Right Said Fred, Wang Chung, or Emerson, Lake, and Palmer.

- References to *Bullwinkle* and other old TV shows, Ginsu knives, or *Schadenfreud* (the German word for the satisfaction obtained from observing the troubles of others).

"He even references his own references," Boss wrote. It was all "part of being a postmodern, self-conscious, deconstructivist, hip kind of host."

At the end of one show, Miller gave his audience a reading list for the next night's program—a list that included T. S. Eliot's poem *The Waste Land*.

Kit Boss: "It was a little weird, a little wild, uh-huh. Like seeing the past, present, and future of television without having to change the channel."

As for Arsenio: "Dennis Miller is the only one who scares me because I have a tremendous respect for him and think he's one of the brightest comics on the scene."

Arsenio need never have feared his new competitor. After a bright start in January 1992, the show faltered and became just another casualty in the late-night sweepstakes; it was canceled in July after a seven-month run.

Miller was philosophical about his short excursion into La-La Land. "I gave it a shot," he told Rick Du Brow in the *Los Angeles Times*. "Crowded field, not enough people watched. At some point, they come up and tap you on the shoulder and you're gone. I thought they tapped me a little quickly."

He analyzed his trouble. "The hardest part is to get guests. People in show business are governed in a large degree by their publicists. And publicists want not to alienate any of the big shows. *The Tonight Show* and *Arsenio* are the big shows now."

As to who was his toughest booking competitor—Leno or Arsenio—Miller replied instantly: "*The Tonight Show*—by light years."

"I'm not naive enough to think that Arsenio Hall

doesn't want to kick my butt. This is the adult world. I don't live in a fairyland. But he did it with a high degree of etiquette. He was classy. He would send me encouraging letters. He gave me nice, encouraging phone calls.

"Whenever he would speak about it in the press, he would mention that he liked the show. Just little things. You know, human things. You knew he was your competitor. He wanted to win. But he handled himself with a reasonable degree of aplomb."

The Tonight Show was "nothing like that," Miller said. "They really wanted to win, more than anything. And I don't think they're in the business of being friendly or displaying that same degree of etiquette that Arsenio did. I'm not the only one saying stuff like that."

As for potential new entries into the talk-show arena—Whoopi Goldberg and Chevy Chase—Miller said: "I don't know that they'll have [the same problems I had] because they're big stars in their own right."

But even with formidable competition like Dennis Miller breathing down his neck, Arsenio never let up on his participation in the war on drug abuse. In January 1992 he was talking to the pastor of his church, Reverend Cecil "Chip" Murray, about a number of crack houses nearby where crack was sold and used. Murray was in the process of urging his congregation at the First AME Church in Los Angeles to donate enough money for the pastor to buy the crack house nearest the church and convert it into a youth center or a place for people to live.

"You shouldn't come out of church and see people walking out with a paper bag through a steel door with a little thing on it," Arsenio said.

Murray and Arsenio continued talking. "That [house] shouldn't be there," Arsenio told Murray. "If I had the money, I'd buy them all."

His own statement gave Arsenio an idea. "If you buy one," he told Reverend Murray, "I'll match it."

And the deal was struck. The church collected the money to buy a nearby crack house, and Arsenio himself bought a second one.

"I now own a crack house, and I'm turning it into a youth center. I hope to buy more until we can get them out of the neighborhoods. I also hope other entertainers with bank [money] would do the same thing."

The crack house Arsenio purchased was located close to Dr. Murray's church. He paid $165,000 for it.

"There are a bunch of them, actually," Arsenio told Oprah Winfrey on her talk show. "I said for every one the church collectively buys, I'll match it. We're in the process of buying up crack houses in the neighborhood."

But the good press about his purchase of the crack house was neutralized by a number of negative stories that came out at about the same time in late 1991.

Story number one concerned the construction of a tennis court about thirty feet in the air above property the news media described as Arsenio Hall's. He was accused of obstructing the views of his prosperous neighbors with an immense tennis court mounted on twenty-five-foot pylons, just a part of a monstrous fifteen-thousand-square-foot mansion he was purportedly building.

"The sad thing is that it isn't even me," Arsenio told *Jet* magazine. "I am an *investor* in the property. I've never *seen* the place. I don't even have a tennis court at my own house. I was just one of the investors. But the media said it was Arsenio's house."

The property referred to is located in the exclusive Hollywood Hills section of Los Angeles.

Story number two had surfaced earlier in 1991.

"The *Los Angeles Times* wrote that I flew over the late Rudy Vallee's home in a helicopter and bought [the house] without seeing it. Other media picked it up."

The story was reprinted far and wide.

The truth of the matter, according to Arsenio, is this:

"I've never been in a helicopter in my life. The *Times* said they were told by a reliable source that I shopped for property by helicopter. I'm even afraid to go on airplanes. But it's cool. It's show business. That story makes me sound like an idiot."

In addition to the helicopter story, there were other rumors involving Arsenio.

"I also read that I was Cher's boy toy," Arsenio said, "and that I wouldn't let Eddie Murphy and a group of his friends into the show. Why can't two men just be friends without people making something out of it?"

That was a rhetorical question.

"This is not going to end until I move back to Cleveland and my career's over," Arsenio sighed. "Our society prefers to feed off negativity."

He elaborated on that on *The Oprah Winfrey Show*. "We flock to ugly negativity and the things that destroy people's lives. And it amazes me. I don't understand it. All the Bird-Cage, *Globe,* and *Star* magazine jokes, and all that kind of stuff. I hate the rags because, once again, it creates a lot of pain for people."

But Arsenio is still positive about his own future. "The whole MTV, BET generation is my audience. I have never tried to compete with Carson. I explained that a million times. Of all the hundreds of reviews, only one was positive when my show first came out. That was the *Hollywood Reporter.*"

For the future: "I want to continue addressing my core audience of youthful, pop-culture blacks and whites who got me where I am. I won't sacrifice them. I have a party every night and you know that there are some white people who just won't come. Some of them just can't get past the color. There are some David Duke supporters who, no matter who I put on, won't watch. I'm going to continue being myself and if some people who are not eighteen to thirty-five but just young at heart, if they can deal with it, come on."

By the end of April 1992, NBC-TV had unleashed a veritable blitzkrieg of promotion on the Johnny Carson–Jay Leno succession. The name Jay Leno suddenly appeared here, there, and everywhere. The overkill in print was at first ignored by Arsenio and his staff, but soon enough the tide of ink spreading Leno's name all over the pages of newspapers and magazines had to be countered.

A thoughtful Arsenio then had this to say about the coronation of Jay Leno to replace the abdicating king:

"I don't think any one man will ever occupy the demographics that Johnny Carson did for twenty-nine years. I think everyone who made up that Carson number will just go everywhere. Some will take up crocheting, some will watch Jay Leno, some will rent more videocassettes. But no one will ever dominate like Johnny."

His stance toughened up shortly after those comments. He also came up with a newsworthy story. On the night of May 22, 1992, Arsenio Hall announced that he would be staying home to watch Johnny Carson's farewell show. In fact, he made plans to telecast reruns for the entire last week of Carson's reign—May 18–22.

"It's a show of respect," he said.

Arsenio made a statement to the stations airing *The Arsenio Hall Show*: "I have a great relationship with my affiliates, and they will trust me once again as they have so many times over the last three years."

Reflecting his toughened attitude, Arsenio had a bit more to say about what would happen to late-night television after Carson's retirement.

"I hear so many people talking about Jay Leno stepping into Johnny's shoes. I think Jay Leno better just step into a new pair of shoes. He can't replace Johnny. No one will ever reign like [Carson] reigned. And I think it's an insult to his legacy to say Jay is replacing him."

And then Arsenio attacked. The target was the constantly reiterated statement that Jay Leno and Arsenio Hall "went back a long way," and that they were "very old friends."

There *were* print verifications of this—from both sides of the fence. In *The Village Voice* in May 1989, Arsenio had said: "We're friends. I give him jokes and he gives me jokes."

In September 1989, *US* magazine quoted Arsenio again: "We would spend hours playing Nintendo together up at his house."

Leno had much to say about Arsenio, too. For example, in the December 1990 *Playboy*: "I taught Arsenio to ride a motorcycle. We used to hang out every night."

Arsenio felt that Leno was playing him for a sucker, mining the friendship, making it appear that Arsenio would graciously make way for the newly crowned king of the late-show mountain without a struggle. And so Arsenio began priming his own publicity batteries. Out came a statement that appeared in *Entertainment Weekly*.

The truth of the matter was, Arsenio said, that even though Jay Leno and Arsenio Hall both started in the business some years before, Arsenio had never called himself a *friend* of Jay's. Not a *real* friend, anyway.

"Jay and I are *not* friends. And you know what? I wasn't anointed, okay? No one put the late-night silver spoon in *my* mouth. I earned every drop of *mine*."

Unlike Jay Leno, who *was* anointed, at least by NBC-TV if not by Carson.

Arsenio assumed a fighting stance. "I'm gonna treat him like we treated the kid on the high school basketball team who was the coach's son. He was there because he was anointed, too. We tried to kick his ass, and that's what I'm going to do—kick Jay's ass. So get ready for me, Jay."

A reprise of this refrain appeared in the June 1992 *Ebony* when Arsenio spoke to Lynn Norment about Leno: "If you put us both in the [Great Western] Forum, I'd blow him out of the fucking building! It would be like the Lakers versus Hollywood High."

Jay Leno said he was stunned by Arsenio's attack on him. He told Rick Du Brow in the *Los Angeles Times*: "I'm genuinely puzzled. I like Arsenio. I think he does a fine show. I've never said anything bad about Arsenio in print, nor have I ever attacked him. He says we're not friends. We were. I mean, I thought we were. He brought his mom in to meet my wife. He sent me an invitation to please come to Hollywood Boulevard when he got his star. I came down. We shook hands. People took pictures."

Poor Jay Leno! When *TV Guide* questioned Arsenio about his sudden attack on his old friend, Arsenio passed it off with: "Feelings get hurt and times change, but I have the utmost respect for Jay as an entertainer—so please, let's move on."

End of the pseudofeud.

For all the brave talk, Arsenio was realistic about the dream of an Arsenio–NBC-TV confrontation in which he could topple *The Tonight Show* from its number-one position.

"There's just too much money and too much inherent power [at NBC]. I know I come off like Muhammad Ali, but at the same time, I'm a very shy, insecure guy. My greatest fear is that my mom and I will be down on the beach selling 'I Used to Be Busy' T-shirts."

Another instance of Arsenio's admitted schizophrenia? Perhaps. Yet, in spite of the fact that Arsenio still talks of himself as one of the most "schizophrenic entertainers" in Hollywood, many of the facts say otherwise. In his challenges to the anointed heir of late-night talk, Arsenio dropped all inhibitions against facing such a formidable competitor. And he was certainly not looking anywhere but straight ahead in his enunciation of policy.

Self-confidence, self-assurance, and a positive attitude toward his life-style and career have resolved many of his inner conflicts—if they ever actually governed his actions. The Arsenio Hall who went full tilt into the fray at the departure of Johnny Carson was in no way the diffident, uncertain, irresolute entertainer who had spent most of his working hours trying to ingratiate himself with the high and mighty of Hollywood.

No more did he worry about who Arsenio Hall was, even though he claimed to have known all along. No more did he worry about offending people in high places—particularly blacks like him who always seemed to come on strong against him. No more did he worry about wounding minorities—like gays, fat people, and other distressed groups. No more did he worry about upsetting the political applecart by being too wild and extravagant, too uptight, or even too politically correct. No more did he worry about persistent questions about the women with whom he associated in his off hours, about raised eyebrows over his men "friends," about his private life in any of its aspects.

Arsenio Hall had become his own man, with no red light coming on suddenly in his mind to warn him off a certain course. Conflicted? Possibly. But only in the way that any one of us is conflicted.

The old ambivalence that he had always sensed in himself and that he had apparently always feared was neutralized now. He had no private reservations on any score. He might, as he once said, have a "heart of gold" one day and the next want to "march with Al Sharpton"—but if he did, he now felt no need to agonize over what direction he would choose. He *knew* the currents and the crosscurrents. He knew how to navigate them with precision and confidence.

As for a "mission in life," he eschewed any big desire to bring off a revolution that would change the world.

"I don't take myself seriously enough to think that I could lead anybody anyplace other than, like, 'The restroom is down the hall on the left.'

"But I would like to try to help any way I can. It's a tough world we live in—crime, recession, drugs, AIDS. If

I could be a guy who for six years, at the end of your day, sends you to bed with a smile on your face, that is a good start.

"I just want to make sure that when I'm gone I've left something or changed something, and that's how I'm living, hopefully, so that, like the old gospel hymn, my living will not be in vain."

Arsenio Hall was by that time established as a star in one of the most difficult milieus of modern times—the entertainment business. And in doing so he was covered with glamorous fallout that guaranteed him permanence in the pantheon of stars.

And the nature of that fallout? Another story may shed light on the particular presence he now exhibited every time he appeared in front of an audience.

Joan Collins, a British B-picture sexpot, made a comeback from a fading career in film when she was assigned the role of the femme fatale Alexis Carrington in the nighttime American television serial *Dynasty,* playing the leading man's ex-wife. Her appearance helped hype the sagging soap and brought it back up near the top of the TV heap.

But the *Dynasty* thing faded and it was on Joan Collins's second comeback—her third sprint, really—that she turned to the stage. In London in 1991 she achieved some dramatic notoriety—or fame—in the starring role in Noel Coward's inexhaustible farce *Private Lives.*

From London Collins went to the United States on tour with the Coward vehicle, and in L.A. agreed to visit *The Arsenio Hall Show.* Heavily made up, the fifty-eight-year-old woman began chatting desultorily about her troubles on the road in handling her twenty-eight pieces of expensive Louis Vuitton luggage, to the snores of millions of viewers and some of the live audience in the studio.

Quickly sensing disaster, Arsenio changed the subject.

"Would you ever wear a 'Heavy D. & the Boyz' T-shirt to bed?" he asked her.

Momentarily some of the audience straightened up. Some of the snorers were diverted enough to open their eyes. The answer was not important. Arsenio clipped merrily on in this new direction.

"I hear that you do splits in your stage show," he told Collins.

Some stamps and squeals. Amused squeals. Nobody believed.

Collins nodded.

"No way I can talk you into doing a split before you leave?" Arsenio said with a cocked eyebrow, meaning that he was telling her to go on and do it.

Collins laughed. "Why not?"

She was dressed in stretch pants and leather boots, not tight skirt or beaded dress. She simply dropped to the floor, one leg out in front, the other out back, toward the set's carpet. Then, thrusting her arm in the air like a teenaged cheerleader, she sank into a perfect split.

The audience went bonkers. Arsenio's posse struck up a funk tune. The dying house party had come alive again.

On her way to the dressing room later, Collins was approached by a curious reporter. Would she do splits for just any talk-show host?

Collins gave an impish smile. "No. This is just for him." As she passed the reporter toward her destination, she turned. "Because this is the sort of thing that works for Arsenio."

Do you have any real way of explaining Arsenio Hall's appeal to the public? the reporter persisted.

Collins shrugged knowingly. "It's stardust."

INDEX

233